23,95

DATE DUE

JUL 2 6 1994		
FEB 19 1997		
APR 1 4 2003		

HIGHSMITH   #LO-45220

D1052902

EFFECTIVE

CONTINUING

EDUCATION FOR

PROFESSIONALS

RONALD M. CERVERO

FOREWORD BY DONALD A. SCHÖN

Effective Continuing Education for Professionals

Jossey-Bass Publishers

San Francisco • London • 1988

EFFECTIVE CONTINUING EDUCATION FOR PROFESSIONALS
by Ronald M. Cervero

Copyright © 1988 by: Jossey-Bass Inc., Publishers
350 Sansome Street
San Francisco, California 94104

&

Jossey-Bass Limited
28 Banner Street
London EC1Y 8QE

Library of Congress Cataloging-in-Publication Data

Cervero, Ronald M.
  Effective continuing education for professionals.

  (The Jossey-Bass higher education series)
  Bibliography: p.
  Includes index.
  1. Professional education — United States.   2. Con-
tinuing education — United States.   I. Title.   II. Series.
LC1072.C56C47   1988   378'.013   88-42782
ISBN 1-55542-127-X (alk. paper)

Manufactured in the United States of America

The paper in this book meets the guidelines for
permanence and durability of the Committee on
Production Guidelines for Book Longevity of the
Council on Library Resources.

JACKET DESIGN BY WILLI BAUM

FIRST EDITION

Code 8848

THE JOSSEY-BASS
HIGHER EDUCATION SERIES

Consulting Editor
Adult and Continuing Education

Alan B. Knox
University of Wisconsin, Madison

CONTENTS

TO Phyllis M. Cunningham
William S. Griffith
Cyril O. Houle

Foreword

THE FAMILY OF activities loosely grouped under the label *continuing education* is already of great importance to the professions and is likely to become even more important as the gap between university-based professional education and the demands of professional practices becomes increasingly apparent. Continuing education needs to be considered as a practice in its own right. We need to ask, as Ronald Cervero does in this useful book, what sets this practice apart from education in general and professional education in particular. We need to ask, as Cervero does, what makes a practitioner of continuing education effective.

Cervero's background suits him for the job he has undertaken. He has had considerable experience as a researcher and practitioner in the field he has chosen to explore, and he appears to be thoroughly familiar with its literature.

Cervero has organized his book around a set of important questions: how professionals learn, what motivates them to avoid or engage in continuing education, what theories underlie programs of continuing education, how the institutional contexts of professional education shape its practice. In each instance, he summarizes what the literature of the field has to offer, then stakes out a position of his own. He is aware of some of the dangers of professionalization — routinization of practice and deference to prevailing ideologies — not only among the beneficiaries of continuing education, but also among its practitioners. He takes the view that the aim of continuing education should be to help professionals develop their ability to reflect in and on their own practice and to become critically aware of the evaluative frames within which their professional knowledge-in-action is embedded. He believes that such a competence is learnable, although it may not be teachable by conventional means.

Cervero's book is programmatic. It is less an analysis of particular examples of educational practice than it is an exposition and critique of prevailing theories. But it raises a set of important questions that practitioners, researchers, and theorists of professional education would do well to consider:

- What kinds of teaching are most likely to be useful to practitioners who wish to enhance their abilities to reflect in and on their practice, to become aware of their own problem-setting frameworks, and to extend their repertoires of images, examples, strategies, and appreciations?
- How, in its pedagogical design, might continuing education effect a marriage of applied science and artistry? How might it help practitioners make use of leading-edge contributions in the sciences relevant to their practice, while at the same time improving their grasp of the kinds of artistry that escape prevailing categories of science and technique?
- What would it mean for continuing educators to address critically important issues of professional ethics, to help practitioners become more aware of ethical dilemmas in their own practice and more courageous and thoughtful in dealing with them?

In his approach to these questions, Cervero is aware of the importance of the changing institutional settings in which continuing education takes place — of the increasing disposition of firms and agencies to create their own programs and of universities to enter the field in new ways. He recognizes, correctly, in my view, that universities must create more effective bridges to the actual experience of professional practice, just as the institutions of practice must learn to achieve a more critical, distanced approach to education.

Continuing education has a great advantage over other educational modalities: It occurs when individuals are most likely to be aware of a need for better ways of thinking about what they do. But the practitioners of continuing education, if they are to exploit their natural advantage, must free themselves from assumptions inherent in their own conventional routines.

In their effort to help practitioners become more reflective, they should begin with themselves.

Cambridge, Massachusetts
August 1988

Donald A. Schön
Ford Professor of
Urban Studies and Education
Massachusetts Institute
of Technology

Preface

THE LEADERS OF professional groups and the public have always assumed that professionals would engage in learning throughout their careers. They were right about this: Professionals learn through books, discussions with colleagues, formal and informal educational programs, and reflection on their daily practices. Since the 1960s, one of these forms of education, formal continuing education programs, has increased dramatically. Although no precise data are available, most knowledgeable observers estimate that billions of dollars are spent annually to provide and to attend such programs. As a result, organized and comprehensive continuing education programs are evident today in management, law, medicine, pharmacy, veterinary medicine, public school education, nursing, the military, social work, architecture, engineering, accounting, librarianship, and many other professions. In fact, most professions now embrace the importance of lifelong professional education.

For many years the continuing education function was filled almost exclusively by individuals who were members of the professions themselves. For example, one would find an engineer in a large manufacturing firm planning the continuing education programs for other engineers in the firm. More often than not this engineer would be an adequate practitioner who was put in the position of training director, where it was believed he could do little harm. In contrast, continuing professional education positions increasingly are being filled by people who have developed track records as effective educators. As in the past, most of these educators are members of the profession for which they develop educational activities. However, many others have been trained in the field of continuing education and may have no prior experience with the profession for which they are working.

Continuing educators in many individual professions have formed professional associations and have developed a literature base about how to do their work. For example, nursing and social work each have a journal devoted exclusively to theory and research in continuing education. A related trend is that in the late 1960s many people began to notice commonalities in the practice of continuing education across the professions. As a result, the term *continuing professional education* has come into widespread use to describe a field of educational practice.

My own history illustrates some of the points just made. In the late 1970s I worked in the educational division of a state medical society. During that time I published several articles in the continuing medical education literature and was involved with an association of continuing medical educators. Subsequently, I have been a faculty member at two universities and have taught a course on continuing professional education to graduate students in adult education, accounting, nursing, social work, and several other professions.

This book rests on the assumption that the practice of continuing professional education overlaps with, but is distinct from, other areas of educational practice. The other areas with which it has most in common are preservice professional education and adult and continuing education. Continuing professional educators perform a variety of roles at the intersection of these two areas. The problem with which this book is centrally concerned is to help improve the practice of these educators. The focus in this book — on helping individuals to be effective educators — may be distinguished from two other books. Cyril O. Houle, without doubt the seminal thinker about continuing professional education, wrote *Continuing Learning in the Professions* (1980) to bring conceptual coherence to the educational endeavors of practicing professionals. Philip M. Nowlen, in *A New Approach to Continuing Education for Business and the Professions: The Performance Model* (1988), has provided a fresh approach to thinking about and organizing professionals' continuing education activities. The starting point for both of these books is the professionals themselves and the entire array of educative activities in which they might engage. By comparison, the starting point in this book is the practice of continuing educators who provide some of these educative activities.

The central goal of *Effective Continuing Education for Professionals* is to identify the elements of effective practice for continuing professional educators. A fundamental assumption is that continuing professional education is itself a field of professional practice, like medicine, law, business, and teaching. As described in the book, most practice situations faced by professionals are characterized by uniqueness, uncertainty, and value conflict. That is, most professional practice situations cannot be understood as the application of standardized knowledge to well-formed problems. Continuing professional educators, like other professionals, generally must make choices about the nature of the problem to be solved, as well as how to solve it. This book addresses the most common and important types of situations that continuing professional educators face, the range of choices open to them, and ways to make these choices. To avoid confusion about who is being discussed when the terms *professional* and *practitioner* are used in the book, those who provide education are labeled *educators, continuing educators,* or *continuing professional educators*. The audience for these educational efforts is referred to as *professionals* or *practitioners*.

Audience

The audience for whom this book will be most useful includes all those engaged in continuing education for the professions. This is a fairly large group because, as pointed out in Chapter One, the professions compose over 25 percent of the work force in the United States, or about 30 million people. Continuing professional educators work in many settings: universities, professional associations, employing institutions, and independent organizations that provide continuing education. For those continuing professional educators who have not been formally trained in education, this book provides access to a broader set of educational resources than they may have encountered in their work with one profession. For continuing educators who are not members of other professions, the book provides an analysis of the special characteristics of professionals that influence the practice of continuing education.

Overview of the Contents

In the opening chapter the book's orientation to both the professions and continuing education is explained. It is important to decide which occupations are to be considered professions in order to clearly identify the clientele for continuing professional education. Three different approaches to making this decision are described, and one is selected as the most appropriate. A rationale for continuing professional education as a distinct field of practice is presented in the chapter's concluding section.

Chapter Two identifies three viewpoints regarding the goals for continuing professional education. These viewpoints are framed around the place of the professions in the larger society and how continuing education fits into this relationship. The understanding of professional practice and the relationship of the professions and society are described for each viewpoint. The implications for educational practice are also discussed. Finally, a case is made that one of these viewpoints should be the overriding goal for continuing professional education.

The focus in Chapters Three and Four is on professionals themselves. In Chapter Three a model of professionals as learners is proposed, based on theories and research from cognitive psychology, Donald Schön's writings on the "reflective practitioner," and theories of the acquisition of professional expertise. Chapter Four identifies several characteristics of professionals and the environment in which they work that influence the extent and nature of their participation in educative activities.

The institutional context of continuing professional education practice is reviewed in Chapters Five and Six. Chapter Five identifies the four major types of providers of continuing professional education, analyzes their relative strengths and weaknesses, and presents their differing understandings of what constitutes effective practice. Chapter Six discusses the types of interorganizational relationships formed in continuing professional education and gives a decision-making framework that seeks to explain why continuing educators form these relationships.

In Chapters Seven and Eight attention is focused on ways to develop and evaluate continuing education programs for professionals. Chapter Seven reviews a number of program planning frameworks, including four cross-professional frameworks, and concludes that individual continuing educators should use their own planning frameworks. Chapter Eight identifies seven different types of evaluation questions that are most often asked in continuing professional education, offers strategies for collecting data to answer these questions, and suggests several criteria by which to decide which question to ask when evaluating a program.

Chapter Nine presents a comprehensive understanding of effective practice for continuing professional educators and ways to improve their current practice.

Acknowledgments

Every human activity has a history and this book is no exception. Its origins may be traced to the time when, near the end of my graduate study, Cyril O. Houle encouraged me to take a position in continuing medical education. This turned into my first practice experience in continuing professional education. In my next position as a faculty member at Northern Illinois University, Phyllis M. Cunningham arranged for me to teach a graduate course on continuing professional education. The teaching of this course, and a similar one at the University of Georgia, has been crucial in the development of many of the ideas in this book.

Sharan Merriam was the person who suggested that I write this book and helped me in its initial stages. William H. Young was a coauthor for a book chapter on the organization and provision of continuing professional education that provided much of the material used in Chapters Five and Six. Steven Murphy was particularly helpful in clarifying my thinking on the professions in Chapter One. Several research associates, particularly Lynn Fletcher, Catherine Zeph, and Joan

Dominick, helped with bibliographic sources, lively personal interchanges, and critical readings of early drafts of the book's contents. Although I cannot name them individually, I need to thank the students in my courses in continuing professional education for challenging me to continually reframe my concepts of effective practice. Finally, I must acknowledge Janna Dresden, whose constant intellectual stimulation, emotional support, and love have enriched this effort in untold ways.

Athens, Georgia   Ronald M. Cervero
August 1988

THE AUTHOR

RONALD M. CERVERO is associate professor in the Department of Adult Education at the University of Georgia. He received his B.A. degree (1973) from St. Michael's College (Vermont) in psychology, his A.M. degree (1975) from the University of Chicago in the social sciences, and his Ph.D. degree (1979) also from the University of Chicago in adult education.

Cervero's main research activities are currently in the field of continuing professional education, with particular emphasis on how professionals learn, evaluation techniques, interorganizational relationships, and the training of continuing educators. He has been chairperson of the North American Adult Education Research Conference (1983), a cofounder of the Midwest Research-to-Practice Conference in Adult and Continuing Education (1982), a member of the executive committee of the Commission of Professors of Adult Education (1986–1988), and a consulting editor for *Adult Education Quarterly*. He has written several book chapters and numerous research articles in the area of continuing professional education, and coedited a Jossey-Bass quarterly sourcebook, *Problems and Prospects in Continuing Professional Education* (1985, with C. L. Scanlan).

Cervero has been an adult education faculty member at Northern Illinois University and assistant executive director of the Illinois Council on Continuing Medical Education.

EFFECTIVE

CONTINUING

EDUCATION FOR

PROFESSIONALS

▼

CHAPTER 1

The Dynamics
of Continuing
Professional Education

THERE CAN BE LITTLE argument that the professions are central to the functioning of American society. They teach our children, manage and account for our money, settle our disputes, diagnose our mental and physical ills, guide our businesses, help many of us mediate our relationship to God, and fight our wars. Their members represent over a quarter of the work force and are the primary decision makers for society's major institutions. The work of professionals is important, not only because of their technical skill, but also because they define to a great extent the problems on which they work. As a result they have the power to define our needs. For example, educators decide what our children will learn as well as how. Physicians decide who is healthy and who is not. The special place of the professions in society results as much from their symbolic leadership as from the application of their technical knowledge and skills.

From the beginning of the move to organize professional groups, both their leaders and the public have assumed that practitioners would continue to learn throughout their working lives. They were right in this assumption: Professionals learn through books, discussions with colleagues, formal and informal educational programs, and the rigors of everyday practice. One of these forms of learning, formal continuing education programs, has increased dramatically in the past quarter century. Although no precise data are available, knowledgeable observers estimate that billions of dollars are spent annually

1

to provide and attend such programs (Eurich, 1985). As a result, organized and comprehensive continuing education programs are evident today in engineering, accounting, law, medicine, pharmacy, veterinary medicine, social work, librarianship, architecture, nursing home administration, the military, nursing, management, public school education, and many other professions.

A great deal of evidence indicates that most professions now embrace the importance of lifelong professional education. For example, medicine, perhaps more than most professions, has recognized this for many years (Meyer, 1975). The president of the Association of American Law Schools recently chided those who seek a solution to the problem of lawyer proficiency by focusing solely on law schools, saying that "legal education is a lifelong process that requires a joint effort by the law schools, the bench and the bar, and individual lawyers" (Vernon, 1983, pp. 559–560). A prominent member of the library profession said that even fifteen years ago the discussion of the term *continuing education* was thought unimportant by leaders of the field. Yet, in 1985, at the first World Conference on Continuing Education, "continuing library education was advocated as an essential element of a librarian's lifetime education" (Stone, 1986, p. 489).

These visions reflect the increasing amount of attention being paid to continuing education in the professions. Many professions have a system of accreditation for providers of continuing education (Kenny, 1985). All fifty states use participation in continuing education as a basis for relicensing members of certain professions. Phillips (1987) lists sixteen professions that are regulated in this way. The future of continuing education appears to be headed toward rapid growth and development. Many people believe that systems of continuing education will be built that rival the preprofessional preparation programs now in existence. The leaders of most professions would probably agree that "what we hardly dare prophesy today will be seen by later generations as efforts to achieve a manifest necessity" (Houle, 1980, p. 302). This increasing attention is seen by many as a positive development for continuing education.

This focus has also magnified the widespread shortcomings in the practice of continuing professional education. Houle does not overstate the problems of continuing education today when he describes this typical program: "Faculty members who can be persuaded to do so give lectures on subjects of their own choosing to audiences they do not know, who have assembled only because they want to put in enough hours of classroom attendance so that they can meet a relicensure requirement" (Houle, 1980, p. 266). Furthermore, these simple activities are expected to improve the performance of professionals whose practices are full of complexities, uncertainty, and conflicting value judgments. Given these conditions, the great concern in the professions with the quality of continuing education should not be surprising.

Continuing Education for the Professions

Due to the increasing attention given to continuing education in the professions, a new field of educational practice has come into existence. This field is becoming increasingly differentiated from the educational practices of preprofessional education. For example, many people think of themselves and are considered by others to be continuing medical educators or continuing engineering educators, when, in fact, they may not have had any experience in the preprofessional education of the groups with whom they work. The evidence for this movement is unmistakable. For example, several journals in North America are devoted exclusively to the theory and research of continuing education for specific professions. There is the *Journal of Continuing Education in the Health Professions*, the *Journal of Continuing Social Work Education*, the *Journal of Continuing Education in Nursing*, and the *Journal of Nursing Staff Development*. In addition, there is a trend for continuing educators in specific occupations to form interest groups within their national professional organizations, such as the American Nurses Association. Other educators choose to form their own associations, such as the Society of Medical School Directors of Continuing Medical Education, the Society for the Advancement of Continuing Education in Ministry, and the National Association of State Judicial Educators.

Within the professions the traditional view has been that the continuing education function must be directed by its own members, while the emerging view is that individuals trained in the field of continuing education have the most appropriate background for this function. While there is an increasing movement toward the emerging view, its adherents are still in a significant minority. One estimate (Griffith, 1985) is that of all the people who perform continuing education functions within the professions, 95 percent have been trained only in the content of their own profession. The remaining 5 percent either have their formal training only in education (4.5 percent) or have been trained both in their profession and in education (.5 percent).

Continuing education for the professions as a field of educational practice is quite young. As such, it is guided by concepts that have not been fully thought through or adequately tested. In fact, many of these concepts are holdovers from the models of preprofessional education, which should not be surprising given the academic background of most educators. However, with the entry of more individuals trained in the field of adult education, increasing attentiveness is being given to models and concepts of educational practice from that field.

The purpose of this book is to identify the elements of effective practice in continuing professional education. By making these concepts explicit, the author intends to stimulate an ongoing analysis and critique of practice. The most effective way to improve practice is for educators to understand the assumptions and principles that guide their work, examine whether they are the most useful ones, and change them when necessary. A small but growing literature base in continuing professional education itself serves as a useful point of departure for analysis. This literature has begun to synthesize the voluminous material that describes the research and practice base of continuing education for the individual professions. The literature in the individual professions additionally constitutes a rich resource for the study and practice of continuing professional education. This material is used selectively to illustrate the major issues that are common in the practice of continuing education across the professions.

As a first step toward analyzing practice, it is necessary to make explicit the approaches being used to understand both the professions and continuing education. There is no commonly accepted way to approach these concepts; thus it is imperative that the assumptions underlying this book be stated for the reader to evaluate.

What Are the Professions?

In order to talk intelligently about continuing education for the professions as a field of practice, the differences between professions and other occupations must be examined. Without making this distinction, educators would be practicing in continuing occupational education or continuing education because their clientele would be undifferentiated from adult learners in general.

The problem of defining professions has a long and controversial history. The earliest effort to define a profession is generally considered to be by Flexner in 1915, and the most recent comprehensive analysis was by Friedson (1986). As anyone who has examined the literature on the professions will readily attest, there is no commonly agreed upon answer to the question of what constitutes a profession. Rather, schools of thought with different approaches yield different answers. Because sociologists are no closer to an accepted definition now than in 1915, many have suggested that it makes no sense to try to define the professions at all. Avoiding a conscious attempt at definition would promote the belief that professions are simply those occupations which have gained professional status. This determination is unacceptable to those who wish to think clearly and systematically about continuing education for the professions. The central tasks are to identify the major approaches to a definition, select one, and provide a rationale for the choice. Three approaches that have been identified in the literature are static, process, and socio-economic.

Static Approach. The oldest definitional approach was pioneered by Flexner, who believed "there are certain objective standards that can be formulated" (1915, p. 902) that distinguish professions from other occupations. He identified the following six characteristics as essential for an occupation to claim professional status. Professions must (1) involve intellectual operations, (2) derive their material from science, (3) involve definite and practical ends, (4) possess an educationally communicable technique, (5) tend to self-organization, and (6) be altruistic. Others over the years have compiled the lists of attributes of a profession (Millerson, 1964; Greenwood, 1957). Today many occupations are still applying these generic criteria to decide whether their occupation is a profession. This is particularly true for occupations that are striving for higher status, such as social work (Rose, 1974), school teaching (Shanker, 1985), nursing (Sleicher, 1981), and early childhood education (Ade, 1982). This is called the *static approach* because objective criteria firmly discriminate between those occupations which are inherently a profession and those which are not. Once this distinction is made, it is unlikely that those which are not could ever develop into professions.

Since the 1960s the static approach has received such criticism that almost no one uses it who seriously studies professions as a concept (Friedson, 1986; Johnson, 1972; Vollmer and Mills, 1966). The major problem with this approach is the persistent lack of consensus about the criteria that should be used to define professions. For example, Millerson (1964) found twenty-three elements that were included in various definitions. Of the twenty-one authors used in his analysis, no single criterion was common to all of them. Furthermore, no two authors agreed that the same combination of criteria should be used to define a profession.

Johnson provides a systematic treatment of the reasons for this lack of consensus (1972, pp. 24–27). In his view the fundamental problem arises at the starting point of this approach, which is that there are "true" professions that exhibit all of the criteria to some degree. The procedure of listing criteria without any explicit theoretical framework means that it is possible to apply particular criteria arbitrarily. The implication for continuing education is that, without any way to agree on the criteria that mark a profession, educators cannot have a clear idea of which occupations are professions and which are not.

Process Approach. Because of the problems inherent in the static approach, a different way of thinking about professions developed in the early 1960s. Hughes put it this way: "In my own studies I passed from the false question 'Is this occupation a profession?' to the more fundamental one, 'What are the circumstances in which people in an occupation attempt to turn it into a profession?' " (Vollmer and Mills, 1966, p. v). This *process approach* came into full flower when Vollmer and Mills used it as the organizing principle for their book on professionalization. This approach differs from the all-or-nothing-at-all style favored in the static approach by viewing all occupations as existing on a continuum of professionalization. Thus, the relevant question became How professionalized is an occupation? It has been argued that all occupations go through a natural sequence in their passage to professional status (Wilensky, 1964), although there is no consensus on this point. Another possibility raised by the process approach is that occupations can deprofessionalize, suggesting that the continuum is not a one-way street. A number of authors have explored this possibility for even the most professionalized occupations such as medicine (Haug, 1975) and law (Rothman, 1984). Kleinman (1984) argues that liberal protestant clergy have deprofessionalized their own role as a response to modernization, secularization, and religious pluralism. They have rejected the idea that ordained clergy are experts in religious matters and have replaced it with a role that accepts egalitarian relationships with lay people. Although the process approach assumes that it is possible for a profession to deprofessionalize, it is generally not viewed as desirable.

An important assumption of the process approach is that no clear-cut boundary separates professions from other occupations. Vollmer and Mills state that professionalization is a process "that may affect any occupation to a greater or lesser degree" (1966, p.2). This is important for continuing professional educators because "all occupations seeking the ideals of professionalization are worthy of sympathetic study . . ." (Houle 1980, p. 27). This approach avoids many of the pitfalls of the static approach because it recognizes the dynamic conditions of contemporary occupational structures. Also, by claiming that professions never reach a point of becoming an ideal profession, the rationale is established for both constant improvement and continuing learning.

Another positive aspect of the process approach is its emphasis on understanding the professions in relation to society. The process approach is based on the premise that the professions are necessary to the smooth and orderly functioning of society. In turn, society provides professionals with relatively high levels of money and status as a way of rewarding their highly valued work (Barber, 1963; Parsons, 1949). However, by stressing the socially functional value of professional activity, this approach does not recognize the social inequalities that are a result of these rewards. These inequalities are usually interpreted as natural and even necessary to support professional work.

Because it does not deal critically with the social and economic consequences of professionalization, the process approach has been criticized as "a distortion of reality because it neglects a historical explanation which indicates that any given reward structure is the result of arrogation by groups with the power to secure their claims . . ." (Johnson, 1972, p. 37). That is, the process approach does not seek to understand the professions in terms of their power in society. By failing to account for the processes by which professions gain and use their power and authority, it does not explain how occupations can come to be viewed as more professionalized.

Friedson (1986) concludes that the difficulties encountered in using the static and process approaches to define a profession stem from the same fundamental problem. Both attempt to treat a profession "as if it were a generic concept rather than a changing historic concept with particularistic roots in those industrial nations that are strongly influenced by Anglo-American institutions" (p. 32).

Socio-Economic Approach. Several theorists (Friedson, 1986; Larson, 1977) argue that occupations in England and the United States have sought to be classified as professions since the late nineteenth century, whereas in western Europe, and even more so in eastern Europe, this activity has been nearly nonexistent. Friedson (1986) notes that the newer occupations of Europe "did not seek classification as professions to gain status and justify a market shelter; such an umbrella title imputing special institutional characteristics to them was not employed to distinguish them" (p. 34). Rather, the status and security of these occupations were gained by other means, such as protections provided by their governments.

Instead of striving to find a scientific concept that would apply to a wide variety of settings, several analysts (Becker, 1962; Friedson, 1986) have concluded that any profession is a "folk concept" that is historically and nationally specific. This approach contrasts dramatically with both static and process approaches in that it assumes there is no such thing as an ideal profession and that no set of criteria is necessarily associated with it. There are only those occupations which are commonly regarded by the general public (folk) as professions and those which are not. As Becker (1962, p. 33) argues: "Such a definition takes as central the fact that 'profession' is an honorific title . . . a collective symbol and one that is highly valued." Thus, a profession is determined by which occupations in a specific society at a given historical time have achieved professional status and privileges.

Although this approach assumes that reality and meaning are socially constructed, it emphasizes that "social construction is not a random process but a political war" (Schudson, 1980, p. 218). Relatively high degrees of social and economic rewards are accorded the winners of this war. Professionalization is the process by which producers of special services constitute and control the market for their services (Larson, 1977). In this process, occupations attempt to negotiate the boundaries of a market for their services and establish their control over it. For this professional market to exist a distinctive commodity must be produced. Unlike industrial labor, most professions produce intangible goods in that their product is inextricably bound to the person who produces it. Therefore, the producers themselves have to be "produced" if their products are to be given a distinctive form. In other words, professionals must be adequately trained and socialized to provide recognizably distinct services. This process has been institutionalized in the modern university, which gives professions the means to control their knowledge base as well as to award credentials certifying that practitioners possess this recognizably distinct type of knowledge. Therefore, an occupation's level of professionalization can be assessed by the extent to which public and political authorities accept its credentials as necessary to provide a specific type of service.

Professions in the United States. One approach to determining which occupations are accepted as professions by the public in the United States has been to use the categories developed by the federal Bureau of the Census (Friedson, 1986; Ginzberg, 1979). Although there is some disagreement about how to use census categories, the debate has been framed in such a way as to produce a least-restricted and a most-restricted approach to defining professional occupations. By presenting both of these approaches, the range of occupations that might be considered as clientele for continuing education for the professions can be delimited.

Much of the literature on census definitions has used the categories as they were defined in the 1970 census. Attention was focused on two major categories: (1) professional, technical, and kindred workers and (2) managers and administrators, except farm workers. Some definitions in the literature use all of the occupations in both categories to represent the professions. Some use "new class" theory to identify the existence of a "professional-managerial class" (Ehrenreich and Ehrenreich, 1977; Gouldner, 1979), while others attempt to formalize the perceptions of the general public (Ginzberg, 1979). These definitions are the least restricted ones commonly used to identify professions in the census data.

Some assumptions must be made when extrapolating these definitions to the most recent census figures, because these two categories were rearranged for the 1980 census. In that census a new category was created: managerial and professional specialty. This classification combined the two previous categories, except that technical occupations were moved to another major category. Because the technical occupations have been used in much of the literature, they are included here.

Applying the least-restricted definition to the 1986 census figures produced an estimate of nearly 30 million professionals in the United States (see Table 1). Some of the more populous occupations, totaling over 1 million practioners, are accountants and auditors, engineers, registered nurses, teachers (except college and university), and health technologists and technicians. This collection of occupations made up 27 percent of the employed work force in 1986. In comparison to the total work force, of which 44.4 percent were women, women made up 43.8 percent of the professions (over 13 million women).

Friedson criticizes this broad definition of the professions because of the great heterogeneity in these census categories in terms of educational background, income, and prestige. In its place he offers a more restrictive definition of the professions. For many of these occupations, particularly in the "executive, administrative, and managerial" category, very few had training or educational requirements that were mandatory. He argues that to be able to identify a reasonably homogeneous group of occupations as professional, a more restrictive criterion is necessary. Friedson proposes that for an occupation to be classified as a profession, some amount of higher education must be a prerequisite to employment. The rationale is that "formal knowledge creates qualification for particular jobs, from which others who lack such qualification are routinely excluded. Such a circumstance is likely to mean that those occupations have developed a coherent organization . . . that succeeds in carving out a labor-market shelter . . ." (Friedson, 1986, p. 59).

Using this criterion (see Table 1), most of the occupations in the "professional specialty" category are included, except for "writers, artists, entertainers, and athletes." Some of the occupations command high prestige and income, such as law and medicine, while others score relatively low in these areas, such as school teaching. Nevertheless, whether high or low in prestige, they have almost a complete labor-market monopoly for their services. In the "executive, managerial, and administrative" category, only three occupations are actually professions, according to Friedson: school administrators, including principals and

Table 1.   Number of Professionals in the United States
Based on the 1986 Census.

Census Categories	Type of Definition	
	Least Restricted[a]	Most Restricted[a]
Managerial and professional specialty		
Executive, administrative, and managerial	12,642	1,884
Officials and adminstrators, public administration	467	
Financial managers	409	
Personnel and labor relations managers	114	
Purchasing managers	100	
Managers, marketing, advertising, and public relations	440	
Adminstrators, education and related fields	500	500
Managers, medicine and health	127	127
Managers, properties and real estate	362	
Management-related occupations		
Accountants and auditors	1,257	1,257
Other	2,192	
Professional specialty	13,911	12,031
Architects	132	132
Engineers	1,749	1,749
Mathematical and computer scientists	631	631
Natural scientists	384	384
Health diagnosing occupations		
Physicians	489	489
Dentists	132	132
Other	107	107
Health assessment and treating occupations		
Registered nurses	1,488	1,488
Pharmacists	162	162
Dietitians	73	73
Therapists	257	257
Other	46	46
Teachers, college and university	639	639
Teachers, except college and university	3,559	3,559

Table 1.   Number of Professionals in the United States
Based on the 1986 Census. (continued)

Census Categories	Type of Definition	
	Least Restricted[a]	Most Restricted[a]
Counselors, educational and vocational	173	173
Librarians, archivists, and curators	212	212
Social scientists and urban planners	312	312
Social, recreation, and religious workers		
Social workers	480	480
Recreation workers	75	
Clergy	285	285
Religious workers	71	71
Lawyers and judges	650	650
Writers, artists, entertainers, and athletes	1,781	
Technical, sales, and administrative support		
Technicians and related support	3,364	2,269
Health technologists and technicians	1,124	1,124
Engineering and related technologists and technicians	937	937
Science technicians	208	208
Technicians, except health, engineering, and science		
Airplane pilots and navigators	79	
Computer programmers	549	
Legal assistants	176	
Other	291	
Total	**29,917** (27.30%)[b]	**16,184** (14.77%)[b]

[a]*Source of definitions:* E. Friedson, *Professional Powers* (Chicago: The University of Chicago Press, 1986). See Chapter 3.

[b]Based on a total of 109,497 people employed in 1986 (numbers in thousands).

Source: U.S. Department of Labor, Bureau of Labor Statistics. *Employment and Earnings*, 1987, *34*, 179–183.

superintendents; health administrators; and accountants. In the technical category, only health, engineering, and science technicians are included; airline pilots, computer programmers, and legal assistants are excluded. These occupations are not considered a profession, according to Friedson, because working in them does not depend on possessing higher education credentials. Applying this more restrictive criterion produces an estimate of 16.2 million professionals in the United States, almost 14 million fewer than produced by the least-restrictive definition.

Without a doubt, professions are an important social reality in American society. While there is no agreement on which occupations constitute that reality, we know its parameters. Somewhere between 16 and 30 million people in this country are given the label of professional by the general public. This book is devoted to the practice of continuing education for this group of occupations.

A Comparative Approach to Continuing Education

In the rapid growth of continuing education, most educators have relied for guidance and models on the distinctive knowledge base and structures of a particular professional group. For example, most physicians, accountants, and lawyers would claim that continuing education should keep them up to date, a concept that is consistent with their preservice training in which they were given large amounts of information to remember for application in their practice setting. By relying on preprofessional training, each profession naturally concludes that its continuing education programs are unique to its own profession.

However, many people have noted the similarities of the continuing education efforts of individual professions in terms of goals, processes, and issues (Cervero and Scanlan, 1985; Houle, 1980; Nowlen, 1988; Stern, 1983b). Thus, the concept of "continuing professional education" began to be used in the late 1960s to describe an identifiable field of study and practice. The early advocates for this *comparative approach* were adult and continuing educators who were struck by the similarities in the educational processes used by the different professions with which they worked. Houle's comparative study of seventeen professions convinced him that "certain dominant conceptions guide all of them as they turn to the task of educating their members and that they tend to use essentially the same kinds of facilities, techniques, and thought processes" (1980, p. 15). The most important rationale for this movement is that the study of similarities across the professions can yield a fresh exchange of ideas, practices, and solutions to common problems.

The comparative approach to continuing education for the professions has a base in the literature as well as in the social organization of educators. Several books (Cervero and Scanlan, 1985; Houle, 1980; Nowlen, 1988; Stern, 1983a), numerous articles (such as Pennington and Green, 1976, and an entire issue of the *Canadian Journal of University Continuing Education*, 1983), and many conference reports (such as Baskett and Taylor, 1980; Haag, 1987) have been published on the topic of continuing professional education. The way in which professional organizations organize themselves reflects an increasing awareness of continuing professional education. For example, two major associations of adult educators (National University Continuing Education Association and American Association for Adult and Continuing Education) have specialized divisions devoted to continuing professional education. Finally, many graduate programs in adult and continuing education have a course or sequence of courses devoted to the special knowledge, skills, and issues necessary for effective practice in continuing professional education.

Field of Educational Practice. Although continuing professional education is a recognizable area of educational practice, its conceptual base is the product of several other fields of study. Concepts, theories, and research from different frames of reference are applied in the practice of continuing professional education. Members of a specific profession are *like all other adults* in that they share basic human processes such as motivation, cognition, and emotions, *like some other adults* in that they belong to a profession, and *like no other adults* in that they belong to a particular profession. Each frame of reference implies important dimensions that need to be taken into account in the practice of continuing professional education. This view recognizes the importance of the structure, issues, and content of preservice preparation and the context of professional practice. However, the shift in emphasis is that this is not the only perspective needed. Information can also be taken from other areas of education in order to offer the strongest conceptual base for practice.

Continuing professional education practice is influenced by the fact that the participants are adults who work in a particular setting. Thus, many of the educational processes used in the continuing education of professionals are the same as those used in adult and continuing education and in human resource development and training. The theory and research in these two areas can do much to inform continuing professional educators. The literature on how adults learn, motivations for learning, and other such topics is abundant (Brookfield, 1986; Knox, 1977; Long, 1983). How to develop, implement, and evaluate programs for adults is the subject of a large literature base (Houle, 1972; Knowles, 1980; Knox and Associates, 1980). (Perhaps the most extensive bibliography on the literature of adult education can be found in Houle's *Design of Education* (1972, pp. 237–302). Because many professionals work in organizations, ranging from the small (five- to ten-person) group to huge corporations, the literature base in human resource development (Nadler, 1980, 1984, 1986) provides a useful set of concepts and procedures for the practice of continuing professional education. Topics such as performance assessment, relating education to performance, and organizational development have been well researched and can be profitably applied to professionals as well as nonprofessionals.

The actual choices made in everyday practice by continuing professional educators are conditioned by an additional set of circumstances and considerations. The participants belong to a profession and, as argued by Schön, "the context of a professional practice is significantly different from other contexts . . ." (1987, p.32). Schön describes the commonalities of professional practice that set it apart from other human endeavors. A community of practitioners

> share[s] conventions of action that include distinctive media, languages, and tools. They operate within particular kinds of institutional settings — the law court, the school, the hospital, and the business firm, for example. Their practices are structured in particular kinds of units of activity — cases, patient visits, or lessons, for example — and they are socially and institutionally patterned so as to present repetitive occurrences of particular kinds of situations. A practice is made up of chunks of activity, divisible into more or less familiar types, each of which is seen as calling for the exercise of a certain kind of knowledge [1987, pp. 32–33].

The professions, whose members account for almost 27 percent of the work force in American society, have a relatively high degree of control and influence in the lives of other people in society. Professionals have central roles in educational, cultural, and health institutions; businesses; and the public policy arenas of federal and state governments. Serious shortcomings in the field of continuing professional education have become apparent as continuing education has come to be viewed as a critical part of lifelong professional education.

This chapter has presented an emerging view of continuing professional education from which the elements of effective practice can be analyzed in the remaining chapters. To build the strongest conceptual base for practice, it is important to blend what we know about adult education and learning, human resource development, the structure and content of preservice preparation, and the context of professional practice.

▼

CHAPTER 2

Conflict Over the Goals of the Educational Process

A NUMBER OF VIEWPOINTS exist on the proper role of the professions in society. They provide a context for thinking about the goals of continuing professional education. Although these viewpoints profoundly affect their work, continuing professional educators often do not acknowledge that their practice is based on them. Awareness of these aims is a necessary component of effective practice. Making the goals guiding continuing professional education explicit can place questions about "what it is, why it is, and what it should be in proper perspective, thereby giving sound and purposeful direction to practice . . . [and] it can provide the necessary framework for examining our key assumptions regarding learners, providers, and the content and process" (Scanlan, 1985, p. 6). Being an effective continuing professional educator requires a clear and explicit recognition of the place of the professions in society. Without this understanding, educators are left without an important tool for making decisions in their daily practice and ultimately for improving their practice.

The Social Context of
Continuing Professional Education

Most people agree that the professions are important to society. But there is a notable lack of consensus, indeed open conflict, about the value of the professional work. The view that the professions play a progressive role in improving society has a long history in British and American cultures. The prevailing perception has been that professionals have an altruistic orientation, seen as a necessary antidote to the excesses of capitalism, whereby the public good rather than self-interest is the principle to be followed. In the early 1960s, the editor of *Daedalus*, the respected journal of the American Academy of Arts and Sciences, claimed with great excitement that "Everywhere in American life, the professions are triumphant. . . . Thorsten Veblen's sixty-year-old dream of a professionally run society has never been closer to realization" (Lynn, 1963, p. 649).

By the late 1960s, however, the public's evaluation of the professions began to shift from approval to disapproval. Where once the virtues of the professions were emphasized, their failings became the center of debate. Visible signs of such debate are still in the newspapers nearly every day. The dramatic increase in medical malpractice suits and the resulting attacks on attorneys by physicians are now commonplace. Sparked by the spate of national reports about the failure of American education, one cannot escape relentless criticism of the teaching profession. The public's perception of professional inadequacies has brought the legitimacy of all professions into serious doubt. This doubt is exacerbated by the relatively elevated economic position that most professions still maintain.

Currently there is a diversity of viewpoints regarding the place of professions in society. Some people remain almost entirely positive in their evaluation of the professions, and see no need to change them in any fundamental way. Others are nearly totally negative, and believe that we would all be better off if the professions would disappear. Many, perhaps most, people find themselves torn between these two perspectives, realizing that the professions will probably always exist, but seeing a need for a redirection of their role in society. As members of society, continuing educators also represent these diverse viewpoints about the professions and society, as do leaders of educational institutions, heads of companies where professionals work, members of licensing boards, and state legislators. In many ways everyone is part of the societal conversation about the proper place of the professions in society.

With such different understandings of the role of professions in society, continuing educators must make a choice about the ultimate ends of their work. Their vision of society and the role of the professions within it are two important criteria upon which their choices must be made. Thus, continuing professional educators must necessarily take a position on the appropriate role of the professions in society. Most often these positions are implicit and it is assumed that everyone in the work situation shares them.

The criteria by which effective practice in continuing professional education is judged involve both means and ends. One criterion of an educational program's success is that its goals are achieved, for example, that engineers learn the newest principles for designing nuclear power plants. If engineers learned these principles, then applied them in designing a power plant, an important criterion for effective practice would have been achieved. The continuing professional educator would have provided the means by which the engineers could improve their performance in designing nuclear power plants. However, this assumes that the power plant should be built. What if the citizens of a nearby town do not want it built? What if there is a choice about building it relatively inexpensively in an area that is prone to earthquakes or in a safer area that would cause more expense because of a lack of underground water? Here choices must be made concerning the ends of professional practice. Should the plant be built? Where should it be built?

Has a continuing professional educator been effective if the engineers learned the new principles and then applied them? Yes, if there was consensus about building that specific nuclear power plant. But given the conflict about the end, one could say that the program was effective for the end of designing nuclear power plants. Those who believe that the plant should not be built could posit that the only effective educational program would have been to focus on the political, economic, environmental, and financial issues involved in building the plant.

Making choices about the ends of professional practice is the norm in contemporary society. What is the appropriate content for the schools? Which profile of a healthy personality should guide counselors, psychotherapists, and psychologists?

These choices all point to the question of what the professions' role should be in making these decisions for the larger society. How much power should professionals be given to make ethical decisions? Ultimately, these are value choices, political choices, about what role the professions should play in society. The practice of continuing professional education is inseparable from these value choices.

The various viewpoints about the relationship between the professions and society can be distilled into three fundamentally different ideas. The *functionalist* viewpoint has deep roots in American social theory and practice, and has the greatest number of adherents in continuing professional education today. This viewpoint is generally positive about the place of the professions in society, in contrast to the *conflict* viewpoint, which is essentially negative. The *critical* viewpoint is the most recent to have crystallized; it shares with the conflict viewpoint a recognition of the problems inherent in professional practice. However, rather than seeking to eliminate the professions, its adherents want to restructure the professions in such a way as to minimize their faults.

While this analytical framework cannot describe these viewpoints in their full richness and complexity, it is hoped that readers will accept this limitation so that the implications for educational practice can be brought into sharper focus. Because these viewpoints involve basic values and assumptions about the characteristics of a good society and the best means to achieve it, it is unreasonable to expect that consensus among continuing professional educators is possible or even desirable.

Functionalist Viewpoint

Functionalism has been the dominant viewpoint in American social science for the past several decades. As such, it should not be surprising that its assumptions and tenets have formed the underpinnings for most people's understanding of the relationship between the professions and the larger society. The functionalist approach posits that the professions are service- or community-oriented occupations that apply a systematic body of knowledge to problems that are highly relevant to the central values of society (Rueschemeyer, 1964, p. 17). This approach stresses the functional value of professional activity for the maintenance of an orderly society.

Professional Practice. The key concept in the functionalist viewpoint is expertise. As described by Schön: "Professional activity consists in instrumental problem solving made rigorous by the application of scientific theory and technique" (1983, p. 21). The two key assumptions are that problems of practice are well formed and unambiguous and that these problems can be solved by applying scientific knowledge. Thus, professionals are seen as possessing a high degree of specialized expertise to solve well-defined problems.

The need for well-defined practice problems is crucial, because, as Moore (1970, p. 56) says:

> If every professional problem were in all respects unique, solutions would be at best accidental, and therefore have nothing to do with expert knowledge. What we are suggesting, on the contrary, is that there are sufficient uniformities in problems and in devices for solving them . . . [and that] professionals . . . apply very general principles, standardized knowledge, to concrete problems.

This assumption is so important that Glazer (1974) uses it to distinguish the major and minor professions. In his view the major professions, such as medicine and law, are characterized by "an unambiguous end — health, success in litigation, profit — which settles men's minds" (p. 346). The minor professions, such as education, social work, and city planning, having shifting and ambiguous ends and thus cannot develop a firm knowledge base.

With well-defined problems to solve, a systematic knowledge base can be developed more easily and applied with greater effectiveness and efficiency. Practice is rigorous to the extent that it uses "describable, testable, replicable techniques derived from scientific research, based on knowledge that is objective, consensual, cumulative, and convergent" (Schön,

1985, p. 61). Schein (1973, p. 39) describes the three essential components to a professional knowledge base:

1. An underlying discipline or basic science component upon which practice rests or from which it is developed.
2. An applied science or "engineering" component from which many of the day-to-day diagnostic procedures and problem-solutions are derived.
3. A skills and attitudinal component that concerns the actual performance of services to the client, using underlying basic and applied knowledge.

Armed with this knowledge, professional practice is seen as essentially technical. The best means (expertise) are selected to solve well-defined problems.

Professions and Society. A functionalist view of society is characterized by consensus, order, and equilibrium. It is assumed that all groups and interests in society share a common set of values. These values form the basis for a consensus about the proper ends of society, just as there is consensus about the ends of professional practice. Existing social structures and institutions must be maintained or changed gradually so as to keep society in equilibrium, thus producing an orderly progression toward a better society. As articulated by functionalism's most well-known proponent, the professions are indispensable to society:

> Many of the most important features of our society are to a considerable extent dependent on the smooth functioning of the professions. Both the pursuit and the application of science and liberal learning are predominantly carried out in a professional context. Their results have become so closely interwoven in the fabric of modern society that it is difficult to imagine how it could get along without basic structural changes if they were seriously impaired [Parsons, 1949, p. 34].

The professions are crucial because they apply their knowledge with an altruistic orientation, rather than in their own self-interest. By being guardians of the central values and institutions of society, there is a compelling logic for expanding the extent of professionalism in society. In the *Daedalus* volume mentioned earlier, Barber (1963, p. 686) said:

> The community orientation characteristic of professional behavior [is] indispensable in our society as we know it and as we want it to be. Indeed, our kind of society can now maintain its fundamental character only by enlarging the scope for professional behavior.

Parsons and Barber illustrate an important characteristic of the functionalist viewpoint: a strong belief in the goodness of society as it is currently constituted.

It is appropriate for professionals to be given extraordinary rights and privileges in their work and social rewards in terms of money and status. This is the bargain that society strikes with professionals in exchange for their highly valued and indispensable role in matters of social importance. Hence, many occupations seek professional status. The result of this professionalization process is that society is improved. This bargain improves society because it helps professions recruit the "best and brightest" to their ranks.

Although most observers note deficiencies in the performance of professionals, the overall evaluation of the professions is positive. There is a strong belief that these deficiencies can be remedied by recruiting more capable people to the professions, improving the knowledge base of the professions, or providing more effective training in professional schools. Friedson (1986) summarizes this optimistic evaluation of the relationship between the professions and society:

> The general tenor of their analyses has represented professions as honored servants of public need, occupations essentially distinguished from others by their orientation to serving the needs of

the public through the schooled application of their unusually esoteric and complex knowledge and skill [p. 28].

Continuing educators' understanding of professional practice and the proper place of the professions in society has important implications for their own efforts.

Educational Implications. With the ends of professional practice being fixed and unambiguous, continuing education performs the instrumental function of helping professionals provide higher quality service to clients by improving their knowledge, competence, or performance. Continuing education thus becomes a technical process and the continuing educator's role is replete with technological responsibility:

> Increasingly, one needs a planned approach to professional development if one's professional competence is to be maintained or enlarged. Continuing education specialists play a major facilitating role in this endeavor. They may assist in the determination of developmental needs of clients, design programs in view of expressed needs, and arrange for their implementation [LeBreton and others, 1979, p. 8].

Prototypical continuing educators seek to develop their skills in using "active principles of learning to help achieve the basic aims of the group with which they work. They become not merely reinforcers of the status quo . . . but the colleagues of all who work to further the power and the responsibility of the vocation" (Houle, 1980, pp. 30–31).

Much of the debate about the process of continuing professional education is carried on within a functionalist framework. For example, as systems of continuing education are being built within the professions, one issue is whether educational programs should always be related in some fashion to the improvement of performance. Some, particularly those who employ professionals, take a strong "yes" position on this question. Others argue that performance should only be one of many possible goals of continuing education, along with changes in knowledge or attitudes. The question of performance for what ends is not usually brought up because it is assumed there is consensus about those ends.

Another issue is whether educational systems should be built on the basis of competitive or collaborative relationships among providers. One side argues that competition drives up quality. Those in favor of collaboration say that they can use scarce resources in an efficient manner to develop the best possible programs. Rarely is the question raised of the ends to which these educational efforts are aiming. (These relationships are examined further in later chapters.)

Conflict Viewpoint

Until the 1960s the professions were understood almost exclusively in a functionalist context. Then, a wide range of criticism began to appear that coalesced into a viewpoint that challenged functionalist thinking. In this view professions are not inherently different from other occupations except that they have secured a monopoly for their services in the marketplace, thereby achieving comparatively high income and status for their members (Johnson, 1972). As Haug (1975) asked: "What then is the difference between a plumber and a urologist? Both require training, both deal with pipes. Both are experts in their own fields. . . . Why should one be considered a professional and the other not?" (p. 211). So it is not knowledge per se that makes professionals different, but rather the monopolization of that knowledge. This monopoly of knowledge in a given area produces an aura of mystery about professional work and promotes myths about its relative difficulty (Haug, 1975, p. 198).

This viewpoint asserts that professions are in conflict with other groups in society for power, status, and money. They use knowledge, skills, and altruism as a form of ideology in their quest for these social rewards. Professionalism is seen as an ideology for controlling an occupation, rather than an ideal end-state toward which all occupations should aspire for the betterment of society.

Professional Practice. The key concept in the conflict viewpoint is power. The importance of professionals in society comes not from their expertise but rather from their "power to prescribe" (Illich, 1977, p. 17). By being able to define their clients' problems and to prescribe solutions, professionals create needs for their services. The mark of a professional is neither long periods of training nor an ethical orientation, but rather having the "authority to define a person as a client, to determine that person's need, and to hand the person a prescription" (Illich, 1977, p. 17). The proponents of this viewpoint argue that most occupations aspire to have this power because its lack makes a worker a mere technician carrying out someone else's directives.

The conflict viewpoint seeks to explode the mystique that professional expertise is composed of special knowledge and skills. When this expertise is critically analyzed it dissolves "into empty claims. The professions are vehicles for the preemption of socially legitimate knowledge in the interest of social control" (Schön, 1983, p. 289). Some observers argue that professional services are inherently disabling to people, particularly those who are convinced that only professional knowledge is capable of solving their problems. Thus, key assumptions of professional remedies — "we are the solution to your problems; you don't know what your problem is; you can't understand the problem or the solution; you can't decide whether the solution has dealt with the problem" (McKnight, 1977, p. 116) — disable people from relying on knowledge of their own.

Perhaps the most severe criticism of professional practice is that it produces the reverse of what it is supposed to provide. This view uses iatrogenisis (doctor-created disease) as a defining example. McKnight (1977, p. 112) asks whether we get more sickness with more medicine, more injustice with more lawyers, more ignorance with more teachers, and more family collapse with more social workers. Obviously this view of the relationship of the professions and society is quite negative.

Professions and Society. Where the functionalist approach sees consensus about the proper ends of society, this second viewpoint assumes there is conflict among various groups in society. Where the functionalist viewpoint stresses the concept of a fluid society open to individual social mobility, the conflict viewpoint sees a system characterized by structured social inequality, in which different groups must fight over a limited number of social and economic rewards. Professionalization has primarily an economic function in society in that it is a means of maintaining this system of social inequality. Because the backbone of inequality in contemporary capitalist societies is the occupational hierarchy, professionalization is a powerful means of moving up in this hierarchy (Larson, 1977). The process of professionalization is where "producers of special services sought to constitute and control a market for their expertise. Because marketable expertise is a crucial element in the structure of modern inequality, professionalization appears also as a collective assertion of social status . . ." (Larson, 1977, p. xvi). Professions reap great social and economic rewards by developing and maintaining a monopoly over special knowledge and skills, which is done by limiting access to professional schools and controlling the credentialing systems that form the basis of licensure and certification.

Professions are inherently conservative rather than progressive because they need to support the most basic assumptions of society in order to retain their position of privilege and status (Galper, 1975). They are incapable of meaningfully criticizing the social order, considered a weakness by proponents of the conflict viewpoint. The problems created by the existence of professions would not be solved by more professionalization, but rather by the decline of professional power. This deprofessionalization would leave professionals without claims of mystery, authority, and deference (Haug, 1975). Professional dominance would be replaced by an expert-client relationship in which knowledge is applied in the context of greater accountability (Rothman, 1984). The dominant position of professionals in the social order should be challenged and society should "sort out privileges that ought to be denounced from privileges that ought to be extended to all workers" (Larson, 1979, p. 625).

Educational Implications. Those holding the conflict viewpoint believe that professional competence is not the main problem to which educational solutions must be addressed. Rather, the problem lies in the oppressive system of which professionals are a part. Continuing educators who subscribe to the conflict approach believe that working with individual professionals is the least effective way to move toward deprofessionalization. They believe that until the system is changed, developing educational interventions to help professionals be more "sensitive" to their clients would be a waste of effort. Until the structure that produces professional power is weakened, professionals will maintain hierarchical relationships with clients. Professionals will continue to be reinforced by their initial training, the institutions in which they work, and even the clients themselves.

Proponents of the conflict viewpoint argue that educational intervention must be at the social-structural level, not at the individual level. The form this intervention would take would be either community activism, community organizing, or liberatory education. The prototypical continuing educator of this viewpoint sees professionals engaged in a class struggle with oppressed groups in society. Some of these educators work with oppressed groups, and through these educational efforts seek to improve the groups' chances for success. These continuing educators work with professions in the same way that Ralph Nader worked with the auto industry, in an adversarial role. There are also small numbers of educators in many professions who work collectively to change the relationship between their profession and society. For example, there are physician-educators who work to make the provision of health care more equitable and there are teachers who seek to change the role that schools play in existing social relations. These attempts to change the system are made through their roles as professionals.

Critical Viewpoint

The functionalist and conflict viewpoints are clearly at odds in their general evaluation of the professions. Yet they are similar in several important respects. Both viewpoints see professionals engaging in a one-way application of knowledge to a given problem. The conflict viewpoint challenges the validity of the problems on which professionals work and the special character of the knowledge used to solve these problems. Nevertheless, its adherents see, as do the functionalists, professionals working on well-formed problems using research-based knowledge.

In the past ten years, another viewpoint has been formulated in reaction to the functionalist and conflict viewpoints. Instead of well-defined problems, this viewpoint assumes that professionals construct the problem from a given situation. It provides evidence that there are conflicting value orientations among members of a profession, in terms of desired societal ends. Because professionals are always making choices about what problems to solve and how to solve them, this approach stresses the need for professionals to be critically aware of the implications of these choices. The use of the term *critical* derives from the current widespread application of critical theory to understanding many areas of human endeavor (Sabia and Wallulis, 1983).

Professional Practice. The key approach in the critical viewpoint is dialectic. This contrasts with the linear application of expertise in the functional viewpoint and the one-way domination of clients by professionals in the conflict viewpoint. The ends and means of professional practice are characterized by a dynamic inner tension and are interconnected like a web. In the other two viewpoints there is a separation and consequent linearity between knowing and doing, professional and client, and means and ends. The critical viewpoint challenges this linear view on two major counts: the notion of a fixed and unambiguous problem and the interconnected basis of professional knowledge.

One often hears professionals claim that most of the problems they see are "not in the book." For example, physicians say that 80 percent of their patients' symptoms do not fit into familiar categories of diagnosis and treatment. Thus, the most difficult part of their practice is to decide which problem needs to be solved. Once this is accomplished, a treatment can be prescribed or a referral made to a specialist. Schön (1987) considers this oft-repeated observation to be central to understanding professional practice:

> In the varied topography of professional practice, there is a high, hard ground overlooking a swamp. On the high ground, manageable problems lend themselves to solution through the application of research-based theory and technique. In the swampy lowland, messy, confusing problems defy technical solution. The irony of this situation is that the problems of the high ground tend to be relatively unimportant to individuals or society at large . . . while in the swamp lie the problems of greatest human concern [p. 3].

Professionals conduct most of their practice in the swamp of the real world where problems do not present themselves as well formed and unambiguous, but rather as messy and indeterminate.

In the swamp the practitioner must find or construct problems from ambiguous situations. Thus, problem setting rather than problem solving is the key to professional practice. Practitioners are always in a dialectical relationship with problems, which are characterized by uniqueness, uncertainty, or value conflict. Take the example of the teacher whose student is having difficulty learning how to read. He may not have had a student with this particular set of problems before, so he considers this case unique. He may also be uncertain about how to think about the cause of the problem: Is there a neurological problem? Is the student not applying herself fully? Is a different language spoken at home? Is the student developmentally delayed? The teacher may also experience conflict between a number of values. For example, in choosing how to teach reading to this child, he may be torn between the views of his teacher colleagues, his graduate school advisors and textbooks, and his own personal experience. Should he not seek counsel from other teachers because of the fear that the student will be labeled as a slow learner? What if the student is a member of a minority group? Does the teacher worry about evaluating students using culturally biased forms of criteria? This teacher is not simply selecting means to clear ends, but also must "reconcile, integrate, or choose among conflicting appreciations of a situation so as to construct a coherent problem worth solving" (Schön, 1987, p. 6).

Another distinguishing characteristic of the critical viewpoint is the nature and source of professional knowledge. It is clear where this knowledge does not come from. At the end of his comprehensive study of the relationship between knowledge and power, Friedson (1986) concludes: "To assume . . . that textbooks and other publications of academics and researchers reflect in consistent and predictable ways the knowledge that is actually exercised in concrete human settings is either wishful or naive" (p. 229). He argues that formal, research-based knowledge is expressed in practice in a way that is considerably modified, even contrary, to its original form. In a study of social work, Baskett (1983) found that the complexity of field-based knowledge and the dynamic environment in which it is used should lay to rest the notion that information taught in professional schools and continuing education is actually used in practice.

So where does professional knowledge come from? Schön (1983) argues: "The practitioner has built up a repertoire of examples, images, understandings, and actions" (p. 138). When a professional is trying to make sense of a situation, she sees it as something already present in her repertoire. This knowledge from her repertoire is not applied in a rulelike fashion, but rather functions as a metaphor or exemplar for helping to define the new situation. Walizer (1986) claims that practitioners "tend to think in terms of specific cases and to make decisions about practice and judgments of individuals based on comparisons with previous, similar experiences" (p. 524). For example, if you ask a teacher how she gets a concept across or handles a classroom problem, you are likely to get a story about a particular class or student.

Professions are in a dialectical, transactional relationship with the situations they find in practice. They are regularly making choices about problems to be solved and generating new information to be used in future situations.

Professions and Society. Both the conflict and functionalist approaches understand the professions as homogeneous communities with shared sets of values that work toward common ends. Those working out of a conflict framework believe that members of a professional community band together to constitute and control a market for their services — their common set of values is predicated on economic self-interest. Those working out of a functionalist framework believe that professional groups share a common set of knowledge and a code of ethics for the purpose of providing high-quality services to people and of working toward the betterment of society. In contrast, the critical viewpoint sees heterogeneity within professions. Individuals hold a variety of identities and have different if not conflicting values about the ends of professional practice. Professions are "loose amalgamations of segments pursuing different objectives in different manners and more or less held together under a common name at a particular period of history" (Bucher and Strauss, 1961, p. 326). This approach shifts attention away from what professionals have in common, such as education, status, and knowledge, to how they use these common characteristics for different social purposes (Murphy, 1986).

Every profession has conflicting values about its role in society. For example, many social workers deliver their services by means of individual casework, intending to improve their clients' ability to deal with their needs. But within the profession some argue that casework is a form of "conservative politics" that reinforces institutions, processes, and ideologies that are destructive to human well-being (Galper, 1975). Social work is considered conservative because its basic assumption is that there is nothing wrong with society and that the problems are those of individuals who cannot adjust to society in some way (Heraud, 1973). Therefore, perhaps the most appropriate form of service would be to engage in community organizing to change the structural conditions that cause poverty.

Law is traditionally seen as a form of altruism in which the legal and judicial systems are the guardians of the rule of law for the benefit of society in general (Rueschemeyer, 1964). In this view judges apply legal principles dispassionately, free of political bias and personal prejudice. Another view believes that the legal system has a vested interest in a given social order and lawyers become supporters of an exploitive system in which only a few benefit (Heraud, 1973). The critical legal studies movement that began in the late 1960s argues that legal decisions are really policy choices and that we should dismiss the idea that law is an objective process (Unger, 1986). This movement has grown to such proportions that most law schools have at least one person with this orientation on their faculty.

Ministers who act on the basis of the traditional Christian doctrine, which focuses almost exclusively on spiritual redemption, believe that their primary role is to help members of their congregation to achieve personal salvation. Liberation theology refutes this basic premise of Christian doctrine: "Liberating communities of faith show no separation between the spiritual and the political. The worth of human life is undivided; spiritual transformation is inextricably tied to social and political transformation" (Welch, 1985, p. 51). Clergy who work out of this tradition consider the political work that is necessary to improve the material conditions of people's lives a fundamental part of their ministry.

The "back to basics" movement of the 1970s and the education reports of the 1980s call for a restructuring of schools to raise the level of literacy necessary to meet the requirements of a high-technology economy. Instead of upholding the social order, as these changes if implemented would do, many call for teachers and administrators to develop a "critical pedagogy" (Greene, 1986) that challenges an oppressive social order. Educators need to address the ethical implications of societal inequalities and the ways in which schools reproduce and legitimize these inequalities (Giroux and McLaren, 1986).

The existence of internal dissension and value conflict within the professions is neither new nor surprising. A good deal of evidence supports the existence of conflict and diversity within the professions (Bucher and Strauss, 1961; Perruci, 1973; Murphy, 1986). Perrucci (1973) found eighteen radical movement organizations representing twelve professions, including medicine, engineering, law, psychology, and social work. These organizations share a common criticism of the role of the professions in society. They argue that it is the professionals' ethical role to ask for whom and for what ends their expertise should be used. Their desire is to move beyond technique and means to an understanding of the kind of society in which one works.

The critical viewpoint accepts the need for the professions because important structures and functions in society depend on their special knowledge and competence. It also recognizes that professionals' "special knowledge is embedded in evaluative frames which bear the stamp of human values and interests" (Schön, 1983, p. 345). In other words, technical expertise cannot be applied in a value-neutral way. Clearly problem solving often requires professional technical expertise. However, decisions are often made that go beyond technical knowledge, such as which problem to solve and which form of knowledge is necessary to solve it. These are the kinds of decisions that call for social constraints on professional autonomy and licensure and should be opened up to public discussion.

Educational Implications. The critical viewpoint argues for the abandonment of the idea that there is consensus about professional quality. Professional quality is often a highly contested issue; not all practitioners in a given profession, or all consumers of their services, agree on what high-quality professional service means. The quality of a physician's service cannot be assessed on the basis of technical expertise alone — we must know the ends to which that expertise is being put. For example, while many heart transplant surgeons have a high level of technical skill, they are criticized by members of their own profession as well as the public for investing so many resources on a single patient while many people cannot afford any health care at all. Is this heart transplant surgeon "good"? Maybe so, but it depends on the criteria used to judge her and there is a lack of consensus about the correct criteria.

All professions have differing or conflicting definitions of quality. Some of these differences are due to disagreements about the means, for example, which accounting procedure should be used or which teaching method characterizes a good teacher. But the most profound disagreements occur concerning the ends of professional practice. For example, what content should be taught in the schools, or who has access to what forms of medical care? As a result, continuing educators are constantly faced with the problem of choosing among different definitions of professional quality.

If there was consensus about professional quality, educators would simply be involved in the technical process of determining the best means to achieve those ends. Because there is a lack of consensus, continuing professional educators must take some responsibility for the content of the programs they plan and deliver. The content chosen for an educational program always reflects a particular concept about the desired ends of professional practice. For example, in planning an in-service education program for science teachers, should only evolutionism be taught or must creationism also be included? For many continuing educators these decisions are uncomfortable because they perceive themselves only as experts about the process, not the content, of education. Yet they are involved in content decisions for every program in which they are involved. The critical viewpoint forces continuing professional educators to recognize that the professions cannot be understood independent of their relationship to the larger society. The actions of professionals have profound consequences for the functioning of society. When continuing educators make decisions about the content of educational programs, they are mediating a particular relationship between the educational profession and society.

So, professionals' knowledge is "embedded in evaluative frames" that reflect a particular vision of society. Likewise, continuing educators' efforts are embedded in the same evaluative frames. Every educational program is a statement of the need for a particular form of technical knowledge, as well as a statement about the proper ends of professional practice. The important educational questions in the critical approach are: Why should professionals have this knowledge? and To what ends will it be put? The most important educational decisions that need to be made, then, are who will decide on the content of the program and on the basis of what criteria.

Necessity for Critical Viewpoint

The functionalist approach emphasizes the need to be skilled in the technical aspects of the educational process. This is obviously important. Much of the rest of this book is devoted to these aspects of continuing professional education practice. However, technical skill is necessary but not sufficient for effective practice in continuing professional education. The conflict viewpoint raises important questions about the ends of professional practice and the role of the professions in society. Here the educational process itself is relegated to secondary status. Most of the attention is focused on the "big picture" and the ultimate outcome of that process, which is the diminution of professional power.

The critical viewpoint offers a comprehensive basis for educational practice because it recognizes the need to deal with both the means and the ends of the educational process. This viewpoint suggests that continuing professional educators must understand ethical and political as well as technical dimensions of their work. This viewpoint can easily be woven into existing approaches to continuing education activities, in which members of a profession are almost always involved. As mentioned in Chapter One, 95 percent of all continuing professional educators are members of the profession for which they are developing programs. These people must be able to address the ends of their educational efforts. In addition, those who have been trained in the process of education alone almost always collaborate with members of the profession for which they are developing educational activities. This collaborative effort can be the means of defining the appropriate ends of the educational process.

Effective practice requires that educators understand the ends of their work and the best means to reach those ends. Continuing professional educators must continually — and critically — examine these means and ends in order to better understand their role and communicate it to the professionals with whom they work, and ultimately to society at large.

▼

CHAPTER 3

How Professionals Learn and Acquire Expertise

LEARNERS ARE AT THE CENTER of every continuing professional education program. While learners are the key actors in this drama, the script has been crafted ahead of time by educators. Like playwrights, educators stage an educational drama on the basis of their model of professionals as learners. This model is rooted in what they believe about how professionals know, how professionals incorporate knowledge into practice, under what conditions professionals learn best, and what role prior experience plays in learning. These models of learning are so deeply embedded in educators' psyches that they tend to act on them implicitly. Occasionally, these private beliefs become public concerns when debates occur in professional education literature about the best way to teach or plan programs for professionals.

Which model of the learner is the best? This is a difficult question if you believe that professionals learn in many ways and that forms of learning differ according to desired ends. The noted psychologist Jerome Bruner accepts these conditions and argues that "there is no completely naturalistic way of resolving the question about what model we want to enshrine at the center of our practice of education. . . . At the heart of the decision process there must be a value judgment about how the mind should be cultivated and to what end" (1985, p. 5). In the previous chapter three ways were proposed of conceiving of professionals and their practice, and it was argued that the critical viewpoint should be "enshrined at the center of our practice" of continuing professional education.

The purpose of this chapter is to construct a model of professionals as learners that is consistent with the critical viewpoint. A key premise of this model is that practice itself and, even more importantly, reflection on that practice are the "freshest and most fruitful sources[s]" (Houle, 1980, p. 45) for professional learning. In their educational planning educators should take into account the ways in which professionals develop knowledge through practice. Educational programs can effectively facilitate learning to the extent that they are consistent with a model of the learner based on this premise.

Although the use of a model for learning based on the critical viewpoint is itself a value choice, a compelling body of evidence supports this approach. Sources of evidence are from the field of cognitive psychology, Schön's writings on the "reflective practitioner," and studies of expertise in three professions. The evidence from these three sources differs in language and areas of emphasis because the sources are so diverse. Yet there are many points of convergence in understanding how professionals acquire knowledge. This chapter reviews the concepts and acquisition of professional knowledge, which result in several educational implications.

Cognitive Psychology

Psychologists have always been interested in how people learn. During the early 1970s the dominant orientation in psychology began to change from behavioristic to cognitive, moving from a focus on observable behavior to the study of mind and how it functions (Shuell, 1986). Much of this research has been done with children and with computers (in the field of artificial intelligence), relatively less with adults. Across these different populations a new consensus has begun to emerge on the nature of learning (Resnick, 1983) that has a direct bearing on how professionals learn and how they can most effectively be taught.

Theories and research from cognitive psychology provide a basic understanding of how professionals develop expertise by describing how the mind works. It is generally agreed that to understand expertise one must clearly account for what knowledge is and how it is learned (Glaser, 1984, 1985; Sternberg, 1985). In the cognitive concepts of learning, the focus is on the acquisition of knowledge and knowledge structures rather than on behavior. The model of the learner is based on the premise that "learning is an active, constructive, and goal-oriented process that is dependent upon the mental activities of the learner. This view, of course, contrasts with the behavioral orientation that focuses on behavioral changes requiring a predominantly reactive response from the learner to various environmental factors" (Shuell, 1986, p. 415).

Cognitive psychologists use schema theory to explain knowledge (Glaser, 1984). This theory describes how acquired knowledge is organized in the mind and how cognitive structures facilitate the use of knowledge in particular situations. In this theory, schemata represent knowledge that we experience — interrelationships between situations and events that normally occur. Schemata are prototypes in memory of frequently experienced situations that people use to construct interpretations of related situations. Schemata are the internal models that professionals use where they face new situations.

Cognitive psychologists have identified a variety of schemata types. One of the most fundamental distinctions is between declarative and procedural knowledge. *Procedural knowledge* is *knowledge that,* while *declarative knowledge* is *knowledge how* (Schuell, 1986). Declarative knowledge is our knowledge *about* things. It is represented in memory as an interrelated network of facts (such as $2 + 2 = 4$) that exist as propositions. Procedural knowledge is our knowledge about *how* to perform, such as producing the correct sum when given an addition problem. It is an open debate about which is learned first, and the answer is an important factor in determining a correct model of the learner. If one believes that knowledge always begins as declarative knowledge (Anderson, 1983), then the transmission of information about a given topic to learners is clearly the method of choice. A contrasting viewpoint is that all knowledge is properly considered as "knowledge how," and that individuals can sometimes transform this knowledge into "knowledge that" (Rumelhart and Norman, 1981, p. 343).

Thus, knowledge is acquired by doing because "expertise comes about through the use of knowledge and not by an analysis of knowledge" (Neves and Anderson, 1981, p. 83).

A key form of procedural knowledge is the manner in which one represents the problem to be solved. Most cognitive psychologists agree that the way a problem is posed determines the way in which it is solved (Getzels, 1979; Glaser, 1984; Sternberg, 1985). Glaser explains that "there are schemata for recurrent situations, and that one of their major functions is to construct interpretations of situations" (1984, p. 100). Although the processes of problem finding and problem solving merge into one another, the actions of thought in problem solving differ depending on whether one begins with an already formulated problem or by creating the problem itself (Getzels, 1979). Problem finding is considered an important component of the model of the learner within the critical viewpoint.

One key assumption of this viewpoint is that learning is cumulative in nature — nothing has meaning or is learned in isolation from prior experience (Shuell, 1986). This assumption has a pedigree dating back to Dewey, who said: "No one can think about anything without experience and information about it" (1933, p.34). If people continually try to understand and think about what is new in terms of what they already know, then an effective cycle of learning exists. Schemata are internal models used when professionals are faced with new situations. One compares the schema with the situation, and if it fails to account for certain aspects, "it can be either accepted temporarily, rejected, modified, or replaced" (Glaser, 1984, p.100). In this way, new knowledge structures are created through everyday experience. For example, continuing educators in a professional association select people to sit on an advisory council that decides on the topics for its annual conference. Each year's experience with the council either confirms one's existing schemata or, because certain problems arise due to who is sitting on the council, causes an alteration in the schemata.

The model of learning in cognitive psychology has important implications for educational interventions in which one wishes to change what professionals know or do. Because learning is an active process, the educator's task involves more than the transmission of information. The educator must take into account professionals' prior knowledge because their understanding and interpretation of the information presented depend on the availability of appropriate schemata. Professionals must be able to test, evaluate, and modify their existing schemata so that some resolution can be achieved between the learners' knowledge structures and the one proposed by the new information. Glaser suggests that an effective strategy for instruction "involves a kind of interrogation and confrontation. Expert teachers do this effectively, employing case method approaches, discovery methods, and various forms of Socratic inquiry dialogue" (1984, p.101). A major goal of this form of instruction is to teach learners how to derive schemata that will be useful in their practice. The professional learns what questions to ask to construct useful schemata, how to test new schemata, and what their useful properties are. The most salient concept from cognitive psychology is consistent with much of what has been described as good practice in teaching adults: "Without taking away from the important role played by the teacher, it is helpful to remember that what the student does is actually more important in determining what is learned than what the teacher does" (Shuell, 1986, p. 429).

Schön's Model of Professional Practice

Schön (1983, 1987) has developed a model of professional practice based on detailed studies of several professions, including architecture, town planning, management, and organizational consulting. This model has been used by others to analyze practice in other professions, such as teaching (Munby, 1987), law (Kissam, 1986), and the ministry (Carroll, 1985), and to suggest new ways of educating professionals (Marsick, 1987; Nowlen, 1988).

Professional Knowledge. Schön calls the dominant understanding of professional knowledge *technical rationality,* in which knowledge is conceived as the basic and applied research that is generated within the university setting. Each profession has a systematic knowledge base with four essential properties: "It is specialized, firmly bounded, scientific, and standardized" (Schön, 1983, p. 23). Professionals select the appropriate information to apply in practice. This concept of knowledge is the basis of the functional and conflict viewpoints (discussed in Chapter Two). While some professionals perform better than others, technical rationality does not adequately describe the forms of knowledge that distinguish the excellent practitioner from the merely adequate one. Thus, Schön argues that technical rationality cannot account for the processes that are central to professional "artistry."

Schön's solution is consistent with the critical viewpoint in which professional practice is characterized by indeterminate situations that must be transformed into determinate ones (that is, situations that the practitioner knows how to solve). To understand the relationship between professional knowledge and artistry, Schön says that "we should start not by asking how to make better use of research-based knowledge but by asking what we can learn from a careful examination of artistry, that is, the competence by which practitioners actually handle indeterminate zones of practice . . ." (Schön, 1987, p. 13). By studying professional artistry in a variety of professional fields, Schön has identified two forms of knowing that are central to professional artistry: knowing-in-action and reflection-in-action. Because the latter is central to artistry, Schön's new model of professional knowledge is called reflection-in-action.

In contrast to the model of technical rationality, which views practice as the application of knowledge, Schön's model assumes that knowing is in the actions of professionals. Most of the spontaneous actions that professionals take do not stem from a rule or plan that was in the mind before acting. Professionals constantly make judgments and decisions, and cannot state the rules or theories on which they were based. Schön calls this process *knowing-in-action* and describes it as "the characteristic mode of ordinary practical knowledge" (Schön, 1983, p. 54). This form of knowing has three properties: (1) professionals know how to carry out certain actions and judgments without thinking about them prior to or during performance; (2) they are not aware of having learned to do these things; and (3) they are unable to describe the knowledge that the action reveals (Schön, 1983, p. 54). It is sometimes possible, by reflecting on actions, to describe the tacit knowledge implicit in them. However, descriptions of knowing-in-action are always *constructions* of reality that need to be tested against observations of actual behavior.

Most situations of professional practice are characterized by uniqueness, uncertainty, and value conflict. Therefore, more often than not, knowing-in-action will not solve a particular problem. Rather, one needs to construct the situation to make it solvable. The ability to do this, to *reflect-in-action*, is the core of professional artistry. Professionals reflect in the midst of action without interruption; their thinking reshapes what they are doing while they are doing it. The goal of reflection-in-action is to change indeterminate situations into determinate ones, and the key to successfully completing this problem-setting activity is to bring past experience to bear on current action.

Through their past experience, professionals have built up a repertoire of examples, images, understandings, and actions (Schön, 1983, p. 138). When practitioners make sense of a situation perceived as unique, what they actually do is see it as something already present in their repertoire. Although present and past situations are not exactly the same, past experience can still make sense of the current situation. When practitioners look at a problem in a new way, its utility can be evaluated by asking (1) whether they can frame the situation in such a way as to make it solvable and (2) whether they value the results. This entire process is achieved in the midst of action: Professionals rethink some part of their knowing-in-action, conduct an on-the-spot experiment to test its utility, and incorporate this new understanding into immediate action.

Acquisition of Professional Knowledge. The knowing-in-action of practitioners is acquired from the research produced by university-based professional schools and from the reflection-in-action undertaken in the indeterminate zones of practice (Schön, 1987, p. 40). Reflection-in-action can generate knowledge to be used in new situations, not by giving rise to general principles, but "by contributing to the practitioner's repertoire of exemplary themes from which, in the subsequent cases of his practice, he may compose new variations" (Schön, 1983, p. 140).

Schön is less certain about how reflection-in-action is acquired and has called for more research on why some people learn it better than others (1983). In putting forth his hypotheses on this question, he argues that people reflect-in-action as a matter of course in their everyday life. Thus, when practitioners learn the artistry of professional practice, they learn new ways of using the kinds of competence they already possess. For example, they bring to a situation the abilities to communicate, experiment, and imitate on which they can build (Schön, 1987, p. 118). While these skills allow professionals to reflect-in-action spontaneously, to improve that ability they must reflect on their reflection-in-action by describing what they did. To the extent that professionals can more consciously describe how they reflect and what that teaches them, they can more readily employ that form of knowing in new situations.

Schön (1987) has written about how this new model of professional knowledge can be used to reshape preservice professional education. Two implications for continuing professional education can be translated from Schön's prescription: "Professional education should be redesigned to combine the teaching of applied science with coaching in the artistry of reflection-in-action" (p. xii). First, the teaching of applied science, which is standard fare in continuing professional education, needs to be based on a model of the learner that is consistent with Schön's views. Second, there is a need to focus directly on the acquisition of reflection-in-action.

Schön believes that the research generated by universities is an important source of information for knowing-in-action. However, this applied science must not stand alone, but must be incorporated with reflection-in-action. Otherwise, it has little chance of becoming part of a practitioner's repertoire. Formal continuing education programs should become a place in which "practitioners learn to reflect on their own tacit theories of the phenomena of practice, in the presence of representatives of those disciplines" (Schön, 1987, p. 321) that are related to their practice situations. This repertoire-building process accumulates and describes exemplars in ways that are useful to reflection-in-action. Typical methods of teaching can promote this process. Teaching "how to think like a lawyer" and using the case method in business education and case histories in medicine connect university-based research and theories into practical ways of knowing.

The second implication — improving professional artistry directly by improving professionals' ability to reflect-in-action — is important not only because it is the basis for professional artistry, but also because reflection-in-action is an important source of knowledge for a professional's repertoire. Becoming aware of the reflection-in-action of practice must become an explicit part of continuing education. This would be addressed by examining the "ways in which competent practitioners cope with the constraints of their organizational settings" (Schön, 1987, p. 322). Professionals would reflect on the frameworks they intuitively bring to their performance. Instructors would teach like coaches, explaining how they would perform under these conditions, demonstrating their own approaches to skillful performance, and reflecting with students on the frameworks that underlie their work.

Theories of Expertise in Three Professions

One result of questioning the basis of professional competence in many professions is that a body of theory and research is developing about the nature of professional expertise that is consistent with the critical viewpoint outlined in Chapter Two. Like Schön, researchers seek to understand expertise by carefully examining professional practice. Studies that have been done of nurses, business executives, and teachers follow. Although these studies were carried out independently with different methods, their conclusions regarding the nature and acquisition of expertise are consistent with the critical viewpoint.

Nurses. Benner (1984) developed a model of expertise in clinical nursing practice based on an intensive study of nurses in actual patient care situations. By uncovering the knowledge embedded in nursing practice, Benner presents "the limits of formal rules and calls attention to the discretionary judgment used in actual clinical situations" (1984, p. xix). Benner focuses on what cognitive psychologists call procedural knowledge and what Schön identified as the indeterminate zones of practice. The central premise of Benner's theory is that "expertise develops when the clinician tests and refines propositions, hypotheses, and principle-based expectations in actual practice situations" (1984, p. 3). Her study identifies six types of practical knowledge: (1) graded qualitative distinctions, (2) common meanings, (3) assumptions, expectations, and sets, (4) paradigm cases and personal knowledge, (5) maxims, and (6) unplanned practices. These forms of knowledge are acquired as nurses move through a five-stage sequence in developing skill in actual nursing situations.

Expert nurses have the perceptual and recognitional ability to make *graded qualitative distinctions* in patient care situations. For example, some nurses learn to recognize subtle physiological changes as early warnings to severe medical conditions such as heart attack or shock. These finely tuned abilities come only from many hours of direct patient care.

Nurses working with common issues in patient care develop *common meanings* about helping, recovering, and coping resources in these situations. These common meanings, which have evolved over time and are shared among nurses, form a tradition. For example, one common meaning is that nurses typically try to develop a sense of "possibility" for their patients, even in the most extreme situations. From having monitored the clinical progress of many similar and dissimilar patients, nurses learn to expect a certain course of events without ever formally stating them. These *expectations,* which usually show up in clinical practice and are not in statements of formal knowledge, determine how clinical situations are perceived and acted upon.

Nurses encounter particular experiences that are powerful enough to stand out as *paradigm cases.* Expert nurses develop clusters of paradigm cases around different patient care issues that guide their perceptions and actions in current situations. This type of knowledge is more comprehensive than any theory because nurses compare past whole situations with current whole situations.

Nurses pass on cryptic instructions, which Benner terms *maxims*, that make sense only if the person already has a deep understanding of the situation. For example, intensive care nurses describe subtle changes in a premature infant's respiratory status that make sense only to those who have had a great deal of experience in these situations.

The nursing role in hospitals has expanded largely through *unplanned practices* delegated by the physician and other health care workers. For example, new treatments that must be administered by physicians are frequently left to nurses because they are present at patients' bedsides on a regular basis. This important form of knowledge is often overlooked because it is not a part of a nurse's formal role. Benner (1984) concludes that "a wealth of untapped knowledge is embedded in the practices and the 'know-how' of expert nurse clinicians . . ." (p. 11), which is not recognized because nurses have failed to systematically record what they learn from their own experience.

These six types of practical nursing knowledge are central to skilled nursing practices. This practical know-how is the difference between novice and expert nurses and is acquired only through experience, which "results when preconceived notions and expectations are challenged, refined, or disconfirmed by the actual situation" (Benner, 1984, p. 3). In learning any area of practice, nurses pass through five levels of proficiency: novice, advanced beginner, competent, proficient, and expert (Dreyfus and Dreyfus, 1986). These levels reflect changes in three general areas of skilled performance. One is a movement away from reliance on abstract principles to past concrete experience in actual clinical situations. In the second, nurses see practice situations more and more as a complete whole and less and less as a compilation of equally relevant bits of information. The third is a movement away from detached observer to involved performer.

Novices have no experience in the situations in which they are expected to perform. Without this experience, they must be given general rules to guide their performance. "But following rules legislates against successful performance because the rules cannot tell them the most relevant tasks to perform in an actual situation" (Benner, 1984, p. 21). Advanced beginners can demonstrate marginally acceptable performance because they have coped with enough real situations to learn the recurring meaningful situational components that Benner terms "aspects of the situation" (1984, p. 22). Competent nurses see their actions in terms of a long-range plan of patient care that dictates which aspects of the situation must be considered and which can be ignored. Proficient nurses, in contrast, perceive situations holistically rather than in terms of situational aspects, and performance is guided by maxims. Because of this ability to recognize whole situations, proficient nurses recognize when an expected normal picture does not materialize and quickly reframe the situation to make it solvable. Expert nurses do not rely on an analytical principle (rule, guideline, maxim) to connect their understanding of the situation to an appropriate action. With an enormous background of experience, they have an intuitive grasp of each situation and zero in on the accurate region of the problem without wasteful consideration of a range of alternative solutions. This developmental model of expertise is situation-specific; experienced nurses who enter a situation in which they have no experience may act like novices if the goals and tools of patient care are unfamiliar to them.

The most important educational implication of this model is that programs need to promote the development of clinical knowledge so that each nurse learns from clinical experience. Different instructional strategies are necessary for each level of proficiency because knowledge is acquired differently at each level. Novices are the most difficult to plan for because they have no experience on which to draw. The best strategy is to make the "aspects of the situation" as explicit as possible and whenever possible to include a clinical component to the program. Advanced beginners and competent nurses have enough experience to allow an instructor to teach "the more advanced clinical skill of judging the relative importance of different aspects of the situation" (Benner, 1984, p. 24). Nurses at the proficient and expert levels benefit most from sharing their experiences, clinical case studies, and opportunities to conduct and participate in research on clinical problems. These nurses could provide case studies from their own practice that illustrate either expertise or a breakdown in performance. By working through these cases, learners begin to make explicit the practical knowledge available in their repertoires, as well as the processes by which they frame the situations they encounter.

Business Executives. An increasing amount of research has taken place in the past several years on the cognitive processes underlying expert performance among business managers and senior executives (Isenberg, 1984; Klemp and McClelland, 1986; Quinn, 1988; Wagner and Sternberg, 1985; Weick, 1983). Although these researchers use different language to describe these processes, such as intuition (Isenberg, 1984), thoughtful action (Weick, 1983), and practical intelligence (Wagner and Sternberg, 1985), the common denominator is their effort to understand expert executives' knowledge and how they use it in real-life situations. A review of Isenberg's work (1984, 1985, 1986) illustrates some of the conclusions of this line of inquiry. Isenberg shares with others an emphasis on understanding what knowledge is and how it is used, with less concern about acquiring knowledge.

Isenberg (1984) studied twelve senior managers who were considered excellent performers. His methods included doing intensive interviews, observing them on the job, and engaging them in exercises in which they recounted their thoughts as they did their work. A major conclusion is that managers seldom use a rational approach. That is, they generally do not formulate goals, assess their worth, evaluate alternative ways of reaching them, then choose the way that maximizes expected return. Rather, thinking and acting are inseparable, linked by "thinking/acting cycles" in which managers develop thoughts about their companies, not by analyzing a problematic situation and then acting, but by thinking and acting in close concert. This implies that action is often part of defining the problem, not just of implementing a solution. This is consistent with Schön's argument that a practitioner's ability to reflect on actions while doing them is essential to professional practice.

The primary sources of an executive's knowledge are mental images, experienced and stored scenarios, rules of thumb, and "repertoires of familiar problematic situations matched with the necessary responses" (Isenberg, 1984, p. 86). These forms of knowledge are acquired through extensive experience in problem solving and implementation, and are stored in memory. Executives perform well in complex situations by retrieving these possible courses of action from memory as a result of recognizing familiar features of the problem situation. Problems are solved through a combination of intuition and calculated deductive thinking. Although both cognitive processes are important, Isenberg considers intuition central to the expertise of business executives.

Intuition is not the opposite of rationality, nor is it a random process of guessing. It is "an important thought process for senior managers to use that is based on very rapid recognition, categorization, and retrieval of familiar patterns" (Isenberg, 1985, p. 185). Managers use intuition in five distinct ways. First, they intuitively sense when a problem exists. Isenberg gives the example of a chief financial officer who forecast a difficult year ahead for the company, and, based on a vague gut feeling that something was wrong, decided to analyze one particular division. He found out that the division heads were talking about a future that was not going to happen and thus were putting the entire company at risk. Second, managers rely on intuition to perform well-learned behavior patterns without being aware of the effort. This is very similar to Schön's knowing-in-action. A third function of intuition is to synthesize isolated bits of information and experience into an integrated picture. This is like Benner's description of the proficient nurse who perceives a whole situation rather than aspects of it. Fourth, some managers use intuition as a check on more deductive and purposeful thinking. Typically, managers work on an issue until they find a match between intuitive and purposeful types of thinking. Finally, managers use intuition to bypass in-depth analysis and move rapidly to arrive at a plausible solution. Used in this way, intuition is an instantaneous process in which a manager recognizes familiar patterns.

Because Isenberg and other researchers have paid less attention to how executives acquire knowledge, they have not been explicit about how knowledge and skills could be fostered through education. But given the focus on the experiential basis of executives' knowledge, many of the strategies suggested in this chapter seem appropriate. Strategies that help executives become more aware of their repertoire of "possible courses of action" and the process by which they think in action should be central to the educational process. Several approaches that have been suggested are the case method, simulation exercises, assessment centers, and asking instructors to act as coaches in helping learners acquire the ability to reflect in action.

Teachers. Of the three professions discussed in this section, the base of research and theory about the structure and acquisition of knowledge is largest for teachers. Several large-scale research efforts have helped to uncover this knowledge (Berliner, 1986; Shulman, 1986; Sockett, 1987), along with several major reviews of the literature (Eisner, 1985; Feiman-Nemser and Floden, 1986; Clark and Peterson, 1986). One strand of this literature is consistent with the critical viewpoint. It has looked at teachers' practical knowledge, that is, those beliefs, insights, and habits that enable teachers to do their work in schools (Feiman-Nemser and Floden, 1986). This viewpoint rejects the notion that researchers have knowledge and teachers have experience. It places teachers' practical knowledge, which is gained through experience, at the center of professional practice. In contrast to academic knowledge, teachers' practical knowledge is time-bound and situation-specific, personally compelling, and directed toward action.

Elbaz (1981, 1983) sought to describe the content, organization, and acquisition of practical knowledge embedded in the practice of one high school teacher. Sarah, the subject of the study, had about ten years' teaching experience and was a "responsible and respected member of the English department of her school" (1981, p. 56). Elbaz studied Sarah using several clinical interviews and observations of her classroom performance.

For Elbaz, teachers' knowledge is in a dynamic relationship with practice in that it shapes practice and is derived from practice: "Teachers' knowledge is broadly based on their experiences in classrooms and schools and is directed toward the handling of problems that arise in their work" (1981, p. 67). The five content areas of Sarah's practical knowlege are: subject matter, curriculum, instruction, self, and milieu. However, Elbaz's typology of the structural forms of this knowledge—rules of practice, principle of practice, and images—provides a particularly useful way to think about professionals' knowledge and its dynamic in use.

Rules of practice are brief, clearly formulated statements prescribing what to do and how to do it in frequently encountered practice situations. Teachers implement these rules by recognizing a situation and remembering the rule. In using a rule of practice, the ends or purposes of action are taken for granted. For example, Sarah has a rule for dealing with a learning-disabled student: "He has my full attention after I finish all the instructions" (Elbaz, 1983, p. 133). In contrast, a *practical principle* is more general than a rule of practice and is used when situations are uncertain. A principle is formed, requiring a teacher to reflect in action in order to turn the principle into effective action. For example, when Sarah talks of trying to make the kids happy to walk into the classroom, she states a principle that governs a variety of practices ranging from unstructured talk to coaching a student for an upcoming exam (Feiman-Nemser and Floden, 1986).

Images capture the teacher's knowledge at the most general level, orienting her overall conduct rather than directing specific actions. These images are personally held mental pictures of how good teaching should look and feel, which the teacher expresses in brief metaphoric statements. The image of a window is used by Sarah to orient her practice. She wants to have a window onto her kids and she wants her own window to be more open. For Elbaz, images are the most important form of knowledge because they express teachers' purposes. Whereas rules and principles direct action in specific situations, images order all aspects of practical knowledge. Images also "extend knowledge by generating new rules and principles and by helping to choose among them when they conflict" (Feiman-Nemser and Floden, 1986, p. 514).

Teachers' practical knowledge cannot be acquired vicariously (such as in teacher preparation courses) but is learned and tested through field experience. "The teacher's knowledge grows out of the world of teaching as he experiences it; it gives shape to that world and allows him to function in it" (Elbaz, 1981, p. 58). Elbaz argues that teachers have no unique, specialized methods with which to develop practical knowledge, but must use their skills of observation, comparison, trial and error, and reflection in practice situations. This view agrees with Schön's in that when professionals learn the artistry of professional practice they learn new ways of using competencies they already possess, such as experimentation and imitation.

Although Elbaz does not provide any specific suggestions for educational planning, she does offer several orienting principles. The key suggestion is that continuing education for teachers must build on what teachers already believe about their work. However, many teachers, like other professionals, do not know what they know, so that a first step would be to help teachers uncover the rules of practice, practical principles, and images that guide their practice. In those programs in which the focus is on researchers' theories, there should be an experientially based component whereby teacher-learners can test (either through actual performance or discussion) the relationship of these theories to their existing store of practical knowledge.

A Model of the Learner

Continuing educators' choice of a model of the learner to use in a given situation is a value choice about the ends they wish to achieve. Basing the model of the learner on the critical viewpoint implies that the primary goal of continuing education should be to improve professional artistry or the professionals' ability to operate in the indeterminate zones of practice. In contrast, a model of the learner based on the functionalist viewpoint stresses the importance of acquiring as much technical knowledge (what cognitive psychologists call "knowledge that") as possible to apply to the problems of professional practice. The educational strategies that flow from the functionalist model are effective in helping students acquire technical knowledge. However, these strategies are appreciably less effective in equipping professionals to operate in the indeterminate zones of practice.

The choice of which model of the learner to use must be situation-specific. Even proponents of the critical viewpoint recognize the need for professionals to learn the results of basic and applied science. This kind of knowledge cannot be ignored in the development of professional artistry. We still know very little about how this type of knowledge is integrated into professional know-how, which forms the basis of professional artistry. Although it is inappropriate to use a model of the learner based on the critical viewpoint in all situations, it should become the dominant model underlying educational practice when the goal is to improve professional artistry.

This model of the professional as a learner is one in which professionals construct an understanding of current situations of practice using a repertoire of practical knowledge that has been acquired primarily through experience in prior real-life situations. This model has implications for what must be learned in continuing education programs in order to develop professional artistry or expertise and discover how it can most effectively be learned.

Two forms of knowing should be fostered through continuing professional education. First, the focus must be on what Benner and Elbaz term practical knowledge and what cognitive psychologists call procedural knowledge or know-how. This is contrasted with what is variously termed academic knowledge, technical rational knowledge, or declarative knowledge, which can be characterized as "knowledge that." Practical knowledge is generally understood as a repertoire of examples, metaphors, images, practical principles, scenarios, or rules of thumb that have been developed primarily through prior experience. Because most professionals are not fully aware of the knowledge in their repertoires, it is as important to help them make this knowledge explicit as it is to help them develop new knowledge.

The second form of knowing that should be fostered is the process by which professionals use their practical knowledge to construct an understanding of current situations of practice. This process of thinking in action has been variously called reflection-in-action (Schön), intuition (Isenberg), or problem finding (cognitive psychologists). Unlike the practical knowledge that is unique to their own practice, the process by which knowledge is used is a universal human cognitive act. Thus, both Schön and Elbaz argue that professionals use similar skills to construct an understanding of situations, both within and outside their practice. The continuing professional educator can help the learner make these processes more explicit and thereby open them up to evaluation and improvement.

The starting point of developing educational strategies to most effectively foster these forms of knowing must be that they can be learned but cannot be taught. As cognitive psychologists remind us, what the learner does is more important in determining what is learned than what the teacher does. In seeking to develop either kind of knowing in an educational context, the key is to provide experientially based methods, such as case studies or Schön's examples of coaching, by which learners can uncover or develop their practical knowledge or the processes by which they use it. In Benner's model, the choice of which educational method to use depends partly on the level of expertise the learners possess. Educators may also be able to help learners acquire this knowledge in the context of their daily practice. Thus, Benner and Schön call for helping learners become researchers of their own practice. Glaser argues for using discovery methods, which can teach students how to ask questions in problematic situations and to test the usefulness of the results of the questions.

The risks in using this model of the learner must be understood and avoided. Educators can glorify professionals' practical knowledge simply because it is the knowledge they use in daily practice. In this way educators can make the mistake of believing that the way things are is the way they should be. Practical knowledge must be justified on the basis of public criteria rather than private ones. Also, while recognizing the primacy of practical forms of knowledge, educators should not dismiss technical knowledge. Rather, in fostering the learning of technical knowledge, educators must focus on ways of integrating it into professionals' repertoires of practical knowledge.

▼

CHAPTER 4

Fostering Greater Participation in Educational Activities

CHAPTER THREE WAS BASED on the assumption that continuing professional educators base their practice on a model of the learner. In addition, educators have a model of professionals as participants, which is implicit in their actions to develop and market educational programs. Embedded in this model are beliefs about the reasons why professionals participate in educative activities and about the personality traits, attitudes, and work conditions that foster participation. There is widespread consensus that the goal of this model is to foster greater participation in all forms of continuing education. Houle writes: "Too few professionals continue to learn throughout their lives. . . . They must be identified and eagerly sought, and this fact permeates and will long continue to permeate the practice of continuing professional education" (1980, p. 303).

The effective facilitation of learning is the goal toward which all continuing professional educators should strive. Learning can only occur, however, when professionals participate in activities that are potentially educative, such as reading, peer review, reflection on practice, and formal courses. In the grand scheme, participation is clearly a means to the end of facilitating learning. But for most educators fostering greater participation has become the central goal. Many forces external to the educator support this emphasis on participation as opposed to learning. There are the legal forces in which participation in continuing education, not demonstrated learning, is used as a basis for recredentialing professionals. There are institutional forces in which educators are judged by the number of professionals who enroll in the programs they plan. Finally, there are a number of complex technical issues that educators must solve to truly determine that professionals have learned as a result of participating in an educational program.

To most effectively foster participation, educators must have a clear concept of the types of educative activities in which professionals can participate and the characteristics of professionals that affect their participation (Knox, 1973; Knox, 1985b). In other words, effective practice is based on an understanding of the what and the why of participation. There is no shortage of answers to these two questions. Houle noted in 1980 (p. 125) that even a quick survey of the literature reveals hundreds of publications related to the extent of participation in continuing professional education, characteristics of participants, topics and methods of educational programs, and reasons for participation. It appears that the growth of this literature has continued unabated; the volume of literature about participation was far greater than on any other topic researched for this book.

Despite the number of investigations and publications, no comprehensive framework exists to integrate this knowledge into a workable model of participation. Good beginnings have been made in several lines of inquiry that may eventually combine into a workable framework. The purpose of this chapter is to identify and describe several characteristics of professionals that influence the extent and nature of their participation in educative activities. The various forms of educative activities in which professionals participate are first described. Next, five factors that have been hypothesized to affect professionals' participation in educative activities are discussed. These are: (1) reasons for and deterrents to participation, (2) professionals' zest for learning, (3) professionals' ages and career stages, (4) the basic settings in which professionals work, and (5) requirements for mandatory participation in continuing education.

Forms of Educative Activities

Many discussions of participation make the assumption that fostering participation is only directed at formal educational activities. Yet, any contact with professionals produces much anecdotal evidence that professionals learn from a variety of activities, only one of which is formal instruction. Because most of the research on the forms of professionals' educative activities has been conducted in the absence of a theoretical framework, there is no way to compare the hundreds of studies describing the educative activities of different professional groups, such as teachers (Arends, 1983), engineers (Cervero, Miller, and Dimmock, 1986), physicians (Barham and Benseman, 1984), and dietitians (Holli, 1982).

To fill this void Houle (1980) developed a typology for organizing the variety of activities that are potentially educative and in which educators should seek to foster participation. He identified three "major and overlapping modes of learning" (p. 31), which he labeled inquiry, instruction, and performance. He describes the mode of *inquiry* as

> the process of creating some new synthesis, idea, technique, policy, or strategy of action. Sometimes this mode is employed in a structured fashion; discussion and encounter groups, seminars, clinics, and guided experiences can be used to help people achieve new ideas or new ways of thinking, though the outcomes of the process cannot be predicted in advance. More frequently in this mode, learning is a by-product (though sometimes an intended by-product) of efforts directed primarily at establishing policy, seeking consensus, working out compromises, and projecting plans . . . [p. 31].

Houle says that the effectiveness of this mode is "blighted by any tinge of didacticism, which destroys the spontaneity of the discovery process" (p. 31).

Instruction is the

> process of disseminating established skills, knowl-
> edge, or sensitiveness. Those who use it assume
> that the teacher (a person, book, or any other
> source) already knows or is designed to convey ev-
> erything that the student will learn. . . . The degree
> of success of the mode of instruction is measured by
> the achievement by the student of goals that
> are usually known to the teacher at the beginning of
> a learning episode — though they may be modified
> during its process [p. 32].

Houle notes that most people think of this mode as being the
only form of education, primarily because it is used so extensively in preservice professional education.

Houle defines the mode of *performance* as

> the process of internalizing an idea or using a prac-
> tice habitually, so that it becomes a fundamental
> part of the way in which a learner thinks about and
> undertakes his or her work. In pre-service pro-
> fessional education, the mode of performance is
> used chiefly in "practical" or clinical teaching,
> where it is inculcated by drill, by close supervision,
> by clinical presentations, and by long continued
> demonstration on the part of those who provide
> instruction. During the years of practice, the mode
> of performance may be fostered by the formal use
> of other modes of learning, but it may also be rein-
> forced by rewards and punishments that require
> individuals and groups to maintain and improve
> their abilities and to avoid obsolescence [p. 33].

After the publication of this typology, Houle (Houle,
Cyphert, and Boggs, 1987) suggested that the term *reinforcement*
would be preferable to the term *performance* in characterizing
this mode of learning because of the ambiguity of using *performance* in two different senses: as a mode of learning and as

a summation of what actually occurs in professional practice.

Although Houle describes these three processes as modes of *learning*, I believe they would be more appropriately conceived as modes of *participation*. A more precise description is that there are types of activities in which professionals participate that are potentially educative. Learning ought to be reserved to describe the processes by which cognitive changes occur in the mind. Participation is an activity that has the potential of producing learning, but it certainly does not guarantee it. Although inquiry may have a greater potential than instruction for facilitating learning, participation is still different from actual learning.

Three studies have empirically tested the adequacy of Houle's typology in categorizing professionals' participation in educative activities. Cervero and Dimmock (1987) tested Houle's typology with staff nurses in a medical center hospital. Kovalik (1986) carried out a similar study with pastors representing seven protestant denominations. Polancic (1987) conducted her study with clinical laboratory scientists in eleven Illinois hospitals. For each study an instrument was used to measure the extent of participation in the totality of educative activities undertaken by the respective professional group. Cervero and Dimmock (1987) used an instrument that had been developed by Bevis (1971, 1972) and contained forty-seven types of activities that are potentially educative, such as "Worked with a committee to make decisions" and "Used a self-teaching device." Kovalik (1986) developed an instrument containing fifty activities that were judged to have educative value, such as "Consulted a theological reference work" and "Reviewed and evaluated own sermons." Polancic (1987) developed a survey instrument composed of seventy-one educative activities, such as "Designed an inventory control procedure" and "Attended professional organization convention." Each study used the statistical procedure of factor analysis to determine whether the number of dimensions underlying the total number of educative activities could be reduced to the three in Houle's typology.

Polancic's (1987) results were most consistent with Houle's typology in that she found that the three modes adequately described the educative activities of clinical laboratory scientists.

Cervero and Dimmock (1987) found that while Houle's typology is complete in its description of nurses' educative activities, the mode of instruction can be differentiated into group instruction and self-instruction. Kovalik (1986) found four dimensions underlying pastors' educative activities, which he labeled self-inquiry, self-instruction, reinforcement, and inquiry/reinforcement. His findings have the most discrepancy with Houle's typology in that pastors engage in the inquiry and instruction modes in a more solitary fashion, hence the prefix self- and the discovery of the combined dimension of inquiry/reinforcement.

These three studies lend validity to the usefulness of Houle's typology in conceptualizing the types of activities in which professionals participate that are potentially educative. All three studies found that professionals engage in the mode of performance/reinforcement, even though the actual activities in each profession are different due to their differing practices. Not surprisingly, each study also found professionals engaged in the mode of instruction, although for pastors and nurses self-instructional activities are a distinct type of activity. Inquiry was clearly found as a major mode for nurses and clinical laboratory scientists, whereas for pastors these forms of activities are initiated and completed on their own.

An important component of understanding professionals as participants involves the types of activities in which they participate that are educative. Houle's typology provides an understanding of these activities that is considerably broader than the common concept of formal instructional programs. One implication is that educators may need to expand the vision of their role in fostering participation. In addition to encouraging participation in the mode of instruction through various marketing strategies, they may need to identify the supports and resources needed by professionals to increase participation in other modes. Continuing educators might analyze whether these supports and resources should be expanded or revised in their own setting and whether they are equally accessible to all professionals in the target audience.

Another way to foster participation in these other modes is to help professionals explore the concepts of their own participation; for example, do people recognize the educative character of all three types of activities? Given the different nature of these types of activities, various strategies are probably needed to foster participation in each of them. The type of institution in which educators work may offer particular advantages or constraints to encouraging participation in one or another mode. For example, employment settings are well suited to activities in the performance/reinforcement mode because that is where practice actually occurs.

Professionals as Participants

The assumption underlying most of the voluminous research on participation is that educators can more effectively foster participation if they better understand what motivates professionals to engage in educative activities. Unfortunately, a theory of motivation does not exist to guide the research in this area. Once again, a number of disparate research findings focus on different aspects of motivation, but there is no mechanism to explain how these aspects collectively affect professionals' decisions to participate in educative activities.

Knox (1985b) has made a beginning in this direction by proposing a framework related to adult participation in intentional learning activities. The cornerstone of the framework is that both "personal and situational influences affect the learner's motivation" (Knox, 1985b, p. 289) to participate in educative activities. The transaction between the individual and external factors contributes to a state of motivational energy to engage in continuing education. As a professional's level of motivational energy increases, the likelihood that she or he would decide to participate in educative activities also increases.

The factors that affect professionals' participation can be grouped into personal or situational categories. The most common analytical strategy in this area of research has been to ask professionals about the reasons for and deterrents to participation. Reasons for participation are viewed as primarily personal factors that contribute to their state of motivational energy. The deterrents to participation include both personal and situational factors that influence the level of motivation. Additional personal factors that are mentioned with some frequency in the literature are an internal zest for learning and age and career stage. Frequently mentioned external factors affecting professionals' motivation to participate are the nature of their practice settings and the extent to which they are required to participate in continuing education. In the following sections each of these factors is described and the research is summarized and evaluated.

Reasons and Deterrents. Many continuing professional educators believe that the information most directly applicable to fostering participation is direct evidence from their target audience about the reasons for and the deterrents to their participation. Educators routinely collect this information by surveying program participants and, less frequently, the potential audience for their programs. With this information in hand, program format, location, content, cost, and other factors can be manipulated to increase the likelihood that professionals will participate in their educational programs. Since this basic impulse is so common, it is not surprising that such a sizable literature has built up. Many studies have been reported about educative participation by the members of individual professions, such as nursing (O'Conner, 1979), pharmacy (Mergener and Weinswig, 1979), and medicine (Richards and Cohen, 1980). Some of this research has been influenced by that done in the general field of adult education, which has been summarized in several places (Brookfield, 1986; Cross, 1981; Knox, 1987).

These studies are much too diverse and numerous to summarize neatly. Many of these studies have substantive or methodological problems that reduce the validity of their findings. The most promising lines of research in the "reasons" literature and in the "deterrents" literature have been selected for discussion, as a way of illustrating what is known about professionals as participants. These lines of inquiry have strong theoretical and methodological bases and have involved several professions, thereby creating a cross-professional knowledge base.

Grotelueschen (1985) and other researchers have developed a fairly extensive body of literature regarding professionals' *reasons* for participation. The centerpiece of this research is the Participation Reasons Scale (PRS), which was developed in the late 1970s (Grotelueschen, Harnisch, and Kenny, 1979a) and has been used to assess the reasons for participation of a number of professions, including judges (Catlin, 1982), physicians (Cervero, 1981), veterinarians (Harnisch, 1980), business executives (Grotelueschen, Harnisch, and Kenny, 1979b), and public health administrators (Macrina, 1982). The current version of the PRS is composed of thirty items with Likert-type response options. The respondents' task is to indicate the relative importance of their reasons for participation in a specific continuing education activity or in continuing education in general.

The scale seeks to identify professionals' reasons in five general areas: (a) professional development and improvement, (b) professional service, (c) collegial learning and interaction, (d) professional commitment and reflection, and (e) personal benefits and job security (Grotelueschen, 1985). Items used with physicians that illustrate these clusters are, respectively: (a) To maintain my current abilities, (b) To help me increase the likelihood that patients are better served, (c) To be challenged by the thinking of my medical colleagues, (d) To maintain my identity with my profession, and (e) To enhance my individual security in my present medical profession.

The value of this line of research is that it is both very rigorous and consistent with anecdotal evidence showing that professionals have traditional and accepted reasons (such as improving professional service) as well as nontraditional reasons (such as personal benefits and job security) for participating in continuing education. The findings in the studies cited substantiate these five reasons as important to professionals' participation in continuing education. The studies show that across the professions the most important cluster of reasons is professional improvement and development, followed by professional service, collegial learning and interaction, professional commitment and reflection, and personal benefits and job security. The research also indicates that the reasons for participation can differ significantly according to the type of profession, the career stage of the professional, and personal characteristics such as the type of practice setting and numbers of years in the profession (Grotelueschen, 1985).

Another line of inquiry has sought to identify the *deterrents* to professionals' participation in continuing education. The instrument developed for this assessment, the Deterrents to Participation Scale (DPS), has been used with various health professionals (Scanlan and Darkenwald, 1984) and with social workers (Akintade, 1985). The DPS has also been adapted for use with adults in general (Darkenwald and Valentine, 1985). The DPS is a forty-item survey instrument with Likert-type response options, in which respondents are asked to consider those times in the past year when they were unable or did not desire to participate in continuing education. Respondents indicate how important each reason was in contributing to their decision not to participate in formal continuing education activities.

Scanlan and Darkenwald (1984) studied a statewide sample of physical therapists, medical technologists, and respiratory therapists, and, using the statistical procedure of factor analysis, found six types of deterrents to participation. Akintade (1985) obtained similar results with two statewide samples of social workers. In Scanlan and Darkenwald's study (1984), the first deterrent was labeled disengagement and reflected a general apathy toward participating in continuing education. The second deterrent denoted a general dissatisfaction with the quality of available programs and was called lack of quality. The third deterrent, family constraints, relates to professionals' extra-occupational responsibilities, such as parenting. The cost of attending programs was the fourth deterrent identified. The fifth type of deterrent was that professionals failed to see the relative worth of participating in continuing education; it was labeled lack of benefit. The sixth reflected the conflicting demands on professionals' work time, particularly scheduling difficulties, and was called work constraints.

Participants' ratings of the importance of these six deterrents were used to predict whether or not they were participants in continuing education programs during the previous year. Taken as a whole these six deterrents were able to predict to a significant degree who did and did not participate during the previous year. In terms of their relative importance in predicting participation, the cluster of reasons in disengagement was most influential, followed in order of importance by cost, family constraints, lack of benefit, lack of quality, and work constraints. Of particular importance to continuing professional educators is that four of the six types of deterrents (lack of quality, cost, lack of benefit, and work constraints) relate to factors that can be dealt with in program development and marketing efforts.

Zest for Learning. Professionals have many personality or attitudinal traits that either foster or inhibit their participation in continuing education. Houle (1980) believes that a category of these traits, which he calls one's zest for learning, is centrally related to participation: "The extent of the desire of an individual to learn ultimately controls the amount and kind of education he or she undertakes" (p. 124).

Houle suggests that active practitioners can be divided into four general groups based on their attitudes toward practice, and that those who have wholly or partially withdrawn from practice to fulfill other roles in a profession constitute a fifth group.

At the upper end of the continuum of active practitioners are the *innovators,* who compose the smallest group of people in any profession. These individuals continually seek to improve their performance and "are attracted to ideas and practices that are still untested" (Houle, 1980, p. 156). Innovators participate extensively in educative activities and are likely to favor sophisticated projects such as structured independent learning and sabbaticals to engage in full-time study.

Pacesetters want to be progressive in their practice but are not usually the ones to be first to try a new idea. They value new ideas, but are also conservative about avant-garde practices. Pacesetters feel strongly about their profession and thus strongly support group instructional activities.

A profession's *middle majority* make up most of those in active practice. Because their numbers are so large, their attitudes range from those who look to the pacesetters for new ideas to those who adopt new practices only after they have become widely accepted. The rate of participation in continuing education varies similarly, from enthusiasm for gaining new information to apathy toward learning and education.

The *laggards* learn only what they must in order to stay in practice: "Their ideas have hardened; their old skills deteriorate and they adopt few new ones" (Houle, 1980, p. 159). Their resistance to learning is high and their chief source of new information is people who wish to sell something to them.

The fifth group of professionals, the *facilitators,* are composed of professors, association executives, government regulators, editors, and others who seek to advance a profession but do not actively practice. Because they are drawn from all four groups of active practitioners, facilitators can possess the traits of any one of those groups in terms of their attitudes and the nature of their participation.

There is some evidence supporting the validity of Houle's categories of professionals. Two studies of the impact of continuing nursing education programs (Cervero, Rottet, and Dimmock, 1986; Ruder, 1987) found that the best predictor of participants' post-program performance was their supervisor's classification of them as a member of one of the four groups of active practitioners. That is, innovators were most likely and laggards were least likely to adopt the content of the educational programs into their own practice. Studies of engineers (Kaufman, 1975; Giles, 1985), pharmacists (Gross, 1976), and teachers (Arends, 1983) also found that professionals' attitudes toward practice are related to the extent and nature of their participation. For example, Kaufman found that engineers who rated challenging work activities as very enjoyable tended to participate in more graduate courses than those who found work activities less enjoyable.

Oddi (1984, 1986, 1987) argues that an important dimension of professionals' zest for learning is the extent to which they possess a trait called self-directedness in learning. This trait is to be distinguished from self-directed learning, which is a self-instructional process in which people set goals, develop and implement a learning plan, and evaluate results. Oddi (1987) suggests that this view of self-directed learning as self-instruction offers too limited a scope for such a complex activity as professionals' learning. Her perspective is that self-directedness in learning is a personality construct of professionals "whose learning behavior is characterized by initiative and persistence in learning over time through a variety of learning modes, such as the modes of inquiry, instruction, and performance" (Oddi, 1986, p. 98).

Oddi (1984, 1986) hypothesizes that three dimensions underlie the extent of one's self-directedness. The first is focused on the professionals' ability to initiate and persist in educative activities without immediate or obvious external reinforcement. The second attribute is the extent to which professionals are open to change. The third dimension is professionals' commitment to learning, the valuing of learning for its own sake. Oddi suggests that these three attributes are interrelated and mutually reinforcing in that "they combine to enable this individual to . . . learn from life, be it via self-planned learning projects, participation in formal and informal group learning activities, or reflection on personal performance" (Oddi, 1986, p. 99).

Oddi developed and validated a scale, the Oddi Continuing Learning Inventory, to measure this trait in professionals (1986). She found a considerable range of self-directedness in her studies with law students, nurses, and adult educators. She also found that those who are more self-directed participate in a greater number of educative activities. In her study of the relationship of nurses' self-directedness to their participation in Houle's modes of learning, Lebold (1987) also found a positive relationship between this personality trait and participation in all forms of educative activities. Nurses who are high in self-directedness tend to participate most in self-instructional activities, followed in order by group instruction, inquiry, and performance.

Both anecdotal evidence and rigorous research support the notion that professionals' participation in educative activities is related to their zest for learning. Those who have a great deal of interest in learning participate in a greater number of activities as well as different types of activities. Although the formal research in this area is relatively limited, continuing professional educators would probably increase their effectiveness by taking the variations of this trait into account when developing educative activities.

Age and Career Stage. The stages of career and life development appear to be important factors in the extent and nature of professionals' participation in educative activities. Although the systematic study of life-span development and its relationship to participation in adult education has burgeoned in recent years (Cross, 1981), "specialized applications of general theory to professions and particularly to the lifelong learning of their practitioners have not yet emerged into a significant body of literature" (Houle, 1980, p. 121). However, the limited body of literature does suggest an important relationship between professionals' age and career stage and educational participation. Because the life-span development theories are framed in terms of both age-related and stage-related differences (Cross, 1981), both facets of professionals' development are considered here.

A nearly universal finding is that older professionals tend to participate in fewer formal educational activities than younger professionals. For example, age has been shown to be negatively correlated to the extent or intent to participate for nurses (Rizzuto, 1983), the clergy (Armstrong, 1983), and educational technologists (Waldon, 1985). However, this negative relationship may not exist for all types of educative activities. Lebold (1987, p. 121) found no systematic relationship between age and participation in inquiry, performance, or self-instructional types of educative activities and a slight positive relationship with group instructional activitites.

Although hundreds of studies show the relationship between age and participation, no framework has been proposed that explains why professionals at different ages participate in more or fewer educative activities. Thus, continuing educators must find it difficult to understand how to use information about the ages of their audience to foster greater participation. In contrast, knowledge about the career stages of the potential audience holds more promise in the quest to foster participation. Theories about the career stages of several professional groups, including professors (Baldwin, 1979), the clergy (Armstrong, 1983), and teachers (Glickman, 1985; Katz, 1972), have been developed. Also, a cross-professional developmental model has been proposed by Dalton, Thompson, and

Price (1977) based on their study of scientists, engineers, accountants, and professors.

The main strength of these theories is that they offer a way to think about the different learning needs that exist at different stages in professionals' careers. The work done by Katz (1972) on teachers' developmental stages is illustrative of the potential value of this information to continuing educators. She suggests that teachers pass through four stages (survival, consolidation, renewal, and maturity) during their careers, and vary greatly in the length of time they spend in each stage. Teachers have a unique set of tasks and associated learning needs at each stage that have implications for the timing and location of educational efforts. For example, during the survival stage teachers need a great deal of support, guidance in specific skills, and insight into the complex causes of students' behavior. The most useful type of educative activity is consultation with senior staff members who are readily available and who know the teacher well. Consultations would generally take place at the work site as opposed to courses or conferences at a different location.

Basic Settings of Practice. Houle (1980, pp. 97–101) suggests that professionals are employed in any one of a number of different types of settings, of which five are the most common. He identifies these settings as entrepreneurial, collective, hierarchical, adjunct, and facilitative. Although only a small amount of systematic research has been done on this topic, it appears that professionals working in each setting have access to different ranges and types of educative activities and may have different types of learning needs. As a result, professionals' work setting is an important factor to consider as continuing educators seek to foster greater levels of participation.

In an *entrepreneurial* setting, practitioners organize, operate, and assume the risk for the work done, offering direct service to clients as they require it. Dentistry is a prime example of a profession that operates primarily in this setting. In a *collective* setting, practitioners work with a group of colleagues who share the goal-setting, organizational, and operational procedures. For example, a library is a setting in which a staff of professionals works together in offering a service. In a *hierarchical* setting, professionals are employed by an institution whose basic mission is identified with that of the profession, such as a principal in a school or a health care administrator in a hospital. In an *adjunct* setting, professionals use their expertise in the service of an institution whose basic mission is different from that of their profession. For example, an industrial corporation may employ attorneys, accountants, architects, and nurses. In a *facilitative* setting, practitioners are no longer engaged in the characteristic work of the profession, but instead aid and advance its progress by working in a university, association, or foundation.

A couple of examples illustrate the influence that different work settings have on professionals' participation in educative activities. Houle (1980, p. 101) points out that in entrepreneurial and adjunct settings, members of a given profession do not regularly come into contact with other members of that profession. In contrast, those in collective or hierarchical settings often have a rich professional environment, in which "shop talk" with colleagues presents many opportunities for learning. In hierarchical settings, such as the officers' corps of the armed services, the structure of authority makes it possible to give a great deal of attention to fostering competence and leadership through educative activities.

Two studies provide some support for these speculations. Barham and Benseman (1984) found lower rates of participation in all forms of educative activities (including group instruction and reading the professional literature) for general practice physicians who were in solo practice or in group practice with fewer than three others (the entrepreneurial setting) than for those in large group practices (collective setting) or in hospitals (hierarchical setting). Gross (1976) found that the type of setting in which pharmacists work influences the extent to which they participate in group instructional activities. Pharmacists who work in hierarchical settings (hospitals) voluntarily participate in continuing education to a greater extent than those working in entrepreneurial settings (such as independent, chain, and discount pharmacies).

Mandatory Continuing Education. Many, if not most, profession-als are required to participate to some extent in continuing education. This implies that professionals would suffer punitive consequences by failing to meet the requirement. However, the severity of the consequences for nonparticipation varies greatly. For example, a professional may (1) lose the right to practice in a state or to practice certain functions, (2) lose membership in an association, (3) forfeit the right to increased compensation, or (4) not be allowed to display a new certificate in place of an old one. The most common use of mandatory continuing educa-tion is as a basis for relicensure and recertification of profession-als (Phillips, 1987). At present all fifty states use participation in continuing education as a basis for relicensing at least one pro-fession, with the standard requirement being in the range of twenty to fifty hours every year (Phillips, 1983).

Although the general belief is that these requirements increase professionals' participation in continuing education, only a handful of studies have sought to examine this question. The strategy used to determine the effect of mandatory continu-ing education has been to study professionals' participation both before and after the implementation of state law requiring par-ticipation. Studies have been done on physicians (Colliver and Osborne, 1985; Stross and Harlan, 1978), health professionals (Hermosa, 1986), and certified public accountants (American Institute of Certified Public Accountants, 1985). There is an unusual similarity in the results, which show that 70 to 75 percent of the members of each profession who participated in formal educational programs reported little or no change after the implementation of mandatory continuing education requirements. The greatest changes occur in the remaining 25 to 30 percent, who may be the laggards described by Houle. These individuals may have to increase their negligible participation to the twenty- to fifty-hour level required by most relicensure programs.

Although mandatory continuing education is touted as an effective way to foster participation, the evidence shows a rela-tively weak effect. In fact, in the only study that examined the overall hours of participation for all members of a profession in a state, Stross and Harlan (1987) found no difference in physicians' participation before and after the implementation of a relicensure law in Michigan. The reason for this finding is that the number of hours physicians spend in educational activities is far in excess of that needed for relicensure. Thus, the marginal increase in participation by the laggards is insignificant in light of the total amount of participation in the state. The impact of mandatory continuing education is further attenuated by the finding that an increasing number of programs are offered statewide when a new law is implemented (Colliver and Osborne, 1985). While some increases in participation may be due to the imposition of mandatory continuing education, continuing professional educators who wish to foster participation would be wise not to expect these requirements to substitute for a thorough knowledge of their potential audience.

Fostering Participation in Continuing Education

No standard approaches or powerful technologies exist that will foster professionals' participation in educative activities in all cases. Rather, when continuing educators develop or market educative activities to a potential audience, they must bring to bear a wide array of knowledge about professionals' motivation to participate. This chapter has offered information on five dimensions that influence the extent to which professionals participate in educative activities and the format and content of those activities. (The five dimensions are (1) professionals' reasons for and deterrents to participation, (2) their zest for learning, (3) their age and career stages, (4) the nature of practice settings, and (5) the extent to which they are required to participate in continuing education.) Future research efforts in this area ought to be guided by a theory, such as Knox's (1985b), that explains the dynamic interaction of at least these five dimensions in creating the motivation to participate in educative activities. Until such a theory is developed and tested, however, continuing educators must rely primarily on their own practical knowledge regarding the variety of influences that affect professionals' motivation to participate in continuing education.

▼

CHAPTER 5

Differing Institutional Approaches to Effective Education

IN A STUDY OF how continuing education programs are financed, a respondent explained why her company did not report cost data on training programs (Weinstein, 1982, p. 263):

> No one asked me to figure out all it cost us to run the management seminar last year, but I was curious. So I listed everything I could think of, including lost salary time. I decided to show it to my supervisor, the director of human resources. He was shocked with what I showed him. He told me to "bury it" and never to let top management see the figures on what our seminars cost this company.

Continuing professional educators work almost exclusively in the context of institutional settings. Although these settings vary in size, complexity, and purpose, they have something in common that the above anecdote vividly illustrates: The institutional context is a major, if not *the* major, determinant of continuing educators' understanding of effective practice. Each organization shapes in powerful ways what continuing educators do and how they do it. For example, the conference coordinator in a for-profit continuing medical education organization knows that she will be judged by the number of conference registrations and the net profit from her educational programs. Her institutional context offers clear and explicit guidelines for her vision of effective practice. To the extent possible, she will perform in ways consistent with this vision. Likewise, the human resources director in a hospital has a vision of effective practice that is shaped by the context in which he works. He knows that he will be judged by how well his programs have improved the performance of the hospital's professional staff. Clearly, there are substantive differences in how these two continuing professional educators define effective practice.

The purpose of this chapter is to examine how continuing educators' practice is shaped by the institutional context. Each specific institution has a unique set of values and resources and a particular history and culture. Continuing professional educators are attentive to these characteristics and guide their practice accordingly. Although each institution is unique, groups of institutions share similar characteristics. For example, continuing professional educators in different universities encounter similar opportunities and constraints in their practice. As a result, universities can be considered a type of provider of continuing professional education.

An overview of continuing professional education providers is followed by a discussion of their strengths and weaknesses. Then the major institutional issues faced by continuing professional educators are explored, along with how the particular context frames its practice regarding these issues.

Educators rarely carry out their work without recognizing what other providers are doing and how other institutions may help or hinder their own practice. As a result the issue of competition and collaboration among providers has become a preoccupation of many continuing professional educators. The decisions educators make about interorganizational relationships have become such an important component of practice that they are discussed separately in the next chapter.

Which Institutions Provide Continuing Professional Education?

In summarizing the contributions of a variety of experts, Houle (1983) offered the following description of continuing professional education:

> At a minimum, continuing professional education
> appears to be a complex of instructional systems,
> many of them heavily didactic, in which people
> who know something teach it to those who do not
> know it. The central aim of such teaching, which is
> offered by many providers, is to keep profession-
> als up to date in their practice [p. 254].

While the providers of these instructional systems are as varied
as they are pervasive, no national repository of statistics exists
that describes the number of providers, the number of participants, or the amount of money spent for continuing professional education (Stern, 1983b; Arnstein, 1983; Suleiman,
1983). Where data are available, the estimates vary so wildly
that one cannot trust any one estimate. Thus, in trying to determine who the major providers are, Stern's advice will have to
suffice: until statistics become available, "the experience of 'old
hands' . . . will be a major resource" (1983a, p. 134).

There is, however, consensus in the literature that the
four major providers are universities and professional schools,
professional associations, employing agencies, and independent
providers (Berlin, 1983; Cross, 1981; Houle, 1980; Lynton,
1983; National University Continuing Education Association,
1984; Nowlen, 1988; Nowlen and Stern, 1981). Other types of
providers that are described in the literature are government
(Lynton, 1983), foundations (National University Continuing
Education Association, 1984), autonomous groups such as
teachers' centers (Houle, 1980), and purveyors of professional
supplies and equipment (Houle, 1980). Within each of the
types of providers many forms and subtypes can be identified.

It is impossible to estimate which types of providers are the
most or the least prominent in either the number of offerings or
the number of participants. Arnstein (1983) notes that while
the rules are reasonably well established for counting participants in continuing higher education, "these rules do not extend to
continuing education when offered by business and professional

societies . . ." (p. 238). Also, the relative importance of each type of provider varies with the individual profession. Whereas universities are major providers in medicine and engineering (Derbyshire, 1983; Griffith, 1983), they are second to professional associations in the field of certified public accountancy (Cruse, 1983) and provide virtually no continuing education in the field of real estate (Bloom, 1983). Thus, even if we knew how many educational programs were offered by each type of provider, it is likely that estimates would vary by profession.

The next sections offer brief descriptions of the four major types of providers and the strengths and weaknesses of each institutional type as a provider of continuing professional education. These characteristics present themselves as both constraints and opportunities for practice in continuing professional education.

Universities and Professional Schools. The provision of continuing education by this institutional type is characterized by great diversity (Nowlen, 1988) in annual numbers of participants (from a few hundred to forty thousand), size of budget (from $30 thousand to $17 million), and staff (from one person to more than fifty). Programs may be sponsored by professional schools, colleges, or departments, or by a universitywide continuing education unit. Houle (1980) describes the various ways in which professional schools and universities relate: "There are many kinds and levels of such schools; some are free-standing and others are parts of larger entities, often universities" (p. 175). A recent development is the sponsorship of these schools by corporations, such as by Arthur D. Little and the Rand Corporation. Eurich (1985) has identified eighteen such "corporate colleges."

The patterns by which higher education organizes its continuing professional education function vary a great deal. The primary difference is whether it is coordinated into a single university function (a centralized administration) or administered separately by individual professional schools (a decentralized administration). An extreme example of the latter approach is that in 1977 a major university had thirty-eight separate administrative units responsible for the provision of continuing education (Houle, 1980, p. 181). A major reason that decentralization is a desirable option for professional schools is that continuing education often generates a revenue surplus, which can be used to fund other projects. The decentralized approach is favored by those who insist that the programming function can be performed only by individuals who are trained in the specific profession. As a consequence of this approach, continuing educators (who are usually members of the profession being served), rather than faculty or clients, tend to be the central figures in the planning process (Fox, 1981). These continuing educators usually believe they understand the problems of their profession, academically and from practice, and do not need to rely on others for programming ideas.

The centralized approach is becoming a more viable option because it can provide programming in a more efficient manner. It seems inefficient for several professional schools at the same university to establish duplicative staffs and facilities. Houle (1980, pp. 182–183) notes that general extension divisions are building up staffs of competent programmers with advanced degrees in continuing education. In contrast to the decentralized approach, faculty members and clients have central roles in the educational planning process (Fox, 1981). Because many people with advanced degrees in continuing education do not have a background in the content area in which they are providing programs, they rely on those who do have this background. Another plus for the centralized arrangement is that more physical resources may be available, such as residential centers, audiovisual materials, and computer-assisted instruction. A hybrid of the centralized and decentralized approaches has been implemented at Pennsylvania State University, where the professional school or department is the locus of the planning effort and technical support is given by a centralized university unit (Toombs and Lindsay, 1986).

Higher educational institutions have a number of strengths as continuing professional education providers. Because of their research orientation, universities are the primary source of knowledge for most professions. It is appropriate, then, that the faculty members who originally develop and present this information should teach it to practitioners through continuing education programs (Smutz, Crowe, and Lindsay, 1986). Universities are experienced with lengthy and complex forms of instruction, as delivered in preservice training (Queeney, 1984), and can provide certification for the successful completion of such instruction (Cruse, 1983; Houle, 1980). Unlike other providers that deliver relatively discrete forms of instruction over a short period of time, universities are more capable of offering lengthy types of learning experiences that lead to continuing education credits.

Unlike most other providers, universities have a large resident staff whose full-time responsibility is instruction (Houle, 1980; Suleiman, 1983). With the decline of the school-age population many of these faculty members have insufficient numbers of preservice students and thus are able to turn their energies to the education of practicing professionals. Another strength is that these institutions ordinarily have more abundant and readily available physical facilities than other providers, such as housing, libraries, meeting rooms, state-of-the-art equipment, and food service (Bloom, 1983; Houle, 1980).

The problems faced by professionals are often complex and require interdisciplinary solutions. For example, members of several professional groups (physicians, attorneys, ministers, counselors) may be involved in a decision to remove life-support systems from a patient. The university is in an excellent position to provide educational programs about this issue for representatives from all of these professions because of the comprehensive makeup of its faculty (Nowlen, 1988; Smutz, Crowe, and Lindsay, 1986). Particularly when programming is done by the centralized approach, an individual professional, such as a social worker, might attend a program that has instructors from medicine and law as well as social work.

Perhaps most important is the perception by most professionals that universities are a credible source of continuing education (Cross, 1981; Cruse, 1983; Suleiman, 1983). The perception that "quality is higher education's most important attribute" (Cross, 1981, p. 7) predominates even among those who believe that higher education is losing its place as a major continuing professional education provider (Stern, 1980; Berlin, 1983).

Higher education has a number of weaknesses as a provider. One is that continuing professional education is not a primary function of higher education institutions. One consequence is that substantial and reliable funding is not generally available (Sneed, 1972). Primarily as a result of the lack of a funding base, "the university as an institution has no independent policy and no independent set of practical guidelines in continuing professional education" (Stern, 1980, p. 22). Thus, the continuing education efforts at any one institution are often uneven because they rely upon an enthusiastic committee member, the ability of the programming staff to convince faculty to teach beyond their normal teaching load, or the presence of grant monies to support special programming. Knox (1982) found that almost all income comes from fees paid by participants, which contributed to instability in the programming unit.

A second consequence of being a marginal university function is that professors view continuing education as ancillary to other work and responsibilities. Knox (1982) found a lack of incentives and rewards for faculty participation in one university's continuing education effort. Yet many faculty members will conduct programs for other providers, including other universities, for higher honoraria. Experimentation at Pennsylvania State University has found that faculty members can be encouraged to be part of their university's continuing education effort when they see promise of joint publications, collaborative research, or opportunities for recognition from their peers (Toombs, Lindsay, and Hettinger, 1985).

Universities generally do not have the ability to link what is taught to practice (National University Continuing Education Association, 1984; Sneed, 1972). Even the continuing education representatives of higher education recognize that universities are separate from professional work settings and thus cannot reinforce what is taught as well as other providers. A notable exception is the "practice integrated learning sequence" developed by the Temple University Office of Continuing Medical Education (Lanzilotti and others, 1986). This office-based educational activity incorporates the actual practice of medicine into a formal educational program, with primary focus on the quality of physicians' practice behaviors.

Several other weaknesses have been cited by a prominent leader among the independent providers of continuing education (Suleiman, 1983). Suleiman notes that universities are generally limited to their own faculty and facilities; are generally insensitive to instructional quality; have only limited ideas about how to price their product; lack proper marketing expertise; have internal organizational characteristics that are not conducive to developing, marketing, and administering programs; and tend to be rooted in traditional approaches to fields of knowledge.

Professional Associations. Nowlen (1988) estimates there are at least three thousand national professional associations. Many more state and local associations either are organized independently or are affiliated with a national body. Typically each profession is represented by at least several associations, while some associations have members from several professions. Professional associations think about and deliver continuing education in considerably different ways, depending on the number of members, the scope of purpose, and the size and structure of staff. In many cases, however, the educational program is defined as having to do with the "accreditation of professional schools or other training programs, the issuance of publications, the sponsorship of conventions and conferences, and the operation of special training programs, such as courses, conferences, workshops, and other activities clearly defined as instruction" (Houle, 1980, p. 172). A study done in 1977 showed that nearly all associations provided some form of continuing education for their members, and about one-third sponsored certificate, licensure, or degree programs (Hohmann, 1980).

One of the major strengths of associations is their ability to secure a wide array of talent, especially from their membership. Other providers are usually limited to members of their own staffs. In contrast, associations include among their membership many, if not most, of the professionals in the field, who can bring a variety of points of view to the educational programming (Houle, 1980; Puetz, 1985; Suleiman, 1983). Additionally, because of "an association's breadth of service and continuity of coverage, its educational program has a special capacity to deliver discrete and not necessarily sequential messages" (Houle, 1980, p. 174). Associations are best at sponsoring conferences that build on this strength, as opposed to programs that require depth of coverage over a relatively long duration. Associations also have direct access to professionals who are seeking continuing education and are usually familiar with their learning needs (Cruse, 1983; Suleiman, 1983). Finally, associations are able to engage in some cost-effective strategies for delivering educational programs. For example, in comparison to private enterprises, associations enjoy a nonprofit status and thus have certain financial advantages, such as reduced postage expenses. Also, programs can be replicated within the levels of an association, thus amortizing the start-up costs over a number of offerings. For example, a program developed at the national level can be used by state and local affiliates for a relatively low cost.

A major weakness of professional associations is the organizational placement of the continuing education function (Hohmann, 1980; Houle, 1980; Puetz, 1985). The educational function is typically shared by different divisions or committees responsible for publications, conventions, and the standard type of educational programs. The effect of this practice is that the educational program division may be responsible for only a few specific programs (for example, short courses, tele-lectures), which may not be considered important by the membership because they can find these programs elsewhere. Continuing educators also are often at a disadvantage when they compete for internal resources with other association divisions, such as one dealing with legislative concerns that have greater public relations value.

A second weakness stems from the role of association staff in carrying out the educational function. Staff members usually cannot take the leadership in programming because they are viewed as subordinate to volunteer committees of association members. Although they would like to have a more substantive role in programming, staff are often viewed as simply "seminar schedulers" (Hohmann, 1980, p. 88). Directors of education tend to be involved in many association responsibilities, limiting their ability to take a leadership role in the program development process (Hohmann, 1980). When educational programming is directed by a board that changes from year to year, long-term planning or future-oriented programming suffers.

Several other weaknesses stem from the nature of professional associations. Suleiman (1983) notes that associations typically lack marketing expertise and have only a limited idea about how to price their product. Associations may lack the physical facilities, such as a meeting space and a library, that are necessary for educational ventures. Finally, Nowlen (1988) argues that associations generally do not engage in interprofessional programming because they lack the political base to use association resources to address other professions.

Employment Settings. Employers such as hospitals, social agencies, business firms, and governments offer a tremendous amount of continuing education to their employees. While estimates of the money spent by employers on the educational function vary, a commonly accepted figure is $60 billion annually (Eurich, 1985, p. 6). This may be compared to the $55 billion spent by all higher education institutions in 1981–82. Although not all of this money is spent on educating professionals, a reasonable hypothesis is that more continuing professional education is offered by employers than by higher education. Shelton and Craig (1983, p. 154) cite recent evidence indicating that at least half of the continuing education in health care is provided by employers, in contrast with other providers, and that "most management education is done by employers and by the training industry." The central task of educators in employment settings is to improve participants' performance with respect to the mission of the agency. The measure of success is the extent to which the problem that gave rise to an educational program has been remedied (Houle, 1980; Kost, 1980; Shelton and Craig, 1983).

The employers' ability to directly assess "specific inadequacies of personal or collective service" (Houle, 1980, p. 186) is perhaps the greatest strength of providing education within employment settings. Unlike any other provider, professionals' performance problems can be directly assessed on a regular basis and used to determine both the need for an educational program and the extent to which the program has made a difference in the workplace. Employers have fairly explicit performance expectations, which, when not met, can provide a powerful stimulus for effective educational programming. Continuing educators in the employment setting are in a unique position to coordinate educational strategies with the daily work of employees, thereby increasing the likelihood that what was learned in a program is applied on the job.

It is possible to involve members of several professions in a learning activity to solve a particular organizational problem. A good example is the hospital setting where increasing morbidity or mortality rates are often due to the collective rather than the individual failure of physicians, nurses, and allied health staff.

Another strength from the employer's viewpoint is the relative convenience of scheduling and the minimization of lost work time due to attendance at programs outside the workplace. However, keeping participants' attention when attending an educational activity at the workplace can present several problems that stem from their proximity to their work. It is difficult for employees to maintain their focus to remain present at an educational program when they believe it is more important to attend to their work.

The relative convenience of on-site training must be balanced against the relatively higher cost. In a national study of providers of adult education and training, Anderson and Kasl (1982, pp. 302–303) found that the average cost of a "participant learning hour" (PLH) was $38 for employers, compared to $5 for colleges and universities and $15 for professional associations. Payment by employers for participants' lost work time (in the form of wages) accounts for some of these cost differences; when this cost is excluded the average cost of a PLH drops to $26. The other major cost difference is that instructors' salaries are much higher for employers ($60 per PLH) than for colleges and universities ($20 per PLH) and associations ($35 per PLH).

Because education is subservient to the main goals of the employment setting, the education function often suffers from a lack of regular and substantial support from the parent body, particularly in difficult financial situations (Houle, 1980). Also, most employers of professionals do not have a senior executive in charge of education. Most often the educational function is merged with the personnel function in a human resource development office. Nowlen (1988, p. 174) points out that one result of this structure is that the quality of educational decision making by employers is no more sophisticated than that of other providers. Their educational planning is likely to be far less proficient than for primary organizational goals, such as providing health care or manufacturing consumer goods. Finally, employers can promote only a limited vision of how to solve a work-related problem through learning activities. As Nowlen (1988, p. 174) notes: "The educational strategy can become as incestuous and self-deceptive as the organizational culture which developed it."

Independent Providers. The providers in this category represent a wide range of institutions and constitute a growing segment of the field (Suleiman, 1983). Some of these providers are operated for profit and others are nonprofit, some are cooperative self-help ventures, and some are philanthropic organizations (Houle, 1980, p. 188). Research organizations and consulting firms such as Arthur D. Little, accounting firms, and manufacturers/suppliers such as IBM often use seminars and conferences to gain exposure to customers and client groups. Publishers are also moving into continuing professional education as another way to serve well-defined audiences to whom they currently provide printed materials. There are also the "privates" (Suleiman, 1983, p. 140), institutions that are organized on a free-standing basis and treat continuing professional education strictly as a business.

The greatest advantage that independent providers have is program development. Suleiman (1983) argues that they can respond quickly to learners' needs, "with good instruction free from problems of faculty involvement, committee approvals, and other political considerations" (p. 138). Most private organizations offer programs nationally, which enables them to amortize development costs over a number of offerings. Because of their flexibility, independent providers have pioneered new formats and methods of instruction that have subsequently been adopted by larger and better established providers of continuing education (Houle, 1980, p. 189).

The independent providers' major weakness is that, in general, they lack an automatic image of quality and thus are less credible to their audiences until they demonstrate otherwise. For example, a program sponsored by a manufacturer is generally suspect until it is clear that the educational format is not simply being used to promote products. Lacking a credible image is a problem partly because continuing professional education is a field that is easy to enter. Many independent providers have exploited either professionals' desire to learn or their need to meet recertification requirements with programs that have promised more than they delivered (Houle, 1980, p. 189).

However, independent providers also have the freedom to create their own image. Unlike universities, which have a deeply rooted image, independent providers can develop an image that is consistent with the educational product they wish to sell. Ironically, a common strategy used to overcome this image problem is having faculty members from higher education institutions as instructors. In about 40 percent of the direct-mail brochures received from independent providers by the University of Chicago's Office of Continuing Education, the instructors were university faculty members (Nowlen, 1988, p. 189).

Because "privates" are a single-item business (education) they are extremely sensitive to downward swings in the economy because no other part of the business can pick up the slack when relatively fewer people attend their programs. They also usually lack the facilities necessary for extensive educational programming, such as libraries and many classrooms.

The major points of this discussion of the distinctive characteristics of the four major providers of continuing professional education are summarized in Table 2. Four categories — constituency, credibility, financing, and resources — are used to make provider comparisons. Although each opportunity and constraint does not operate as described for all situations, the table may still be used as a guide for analyzing specific institutional contexts.

Table 2. Distinctive Characteristics of Continuing Professional Education Providers.

Providers	Universities and Professional Schools	Professional Associations	Employers	Independent Providers
Opportunities	*Constituency* · alumni are potential audience *Credibility* · primary source of research and theory · able to credential *Financing* · nonprofit status *Resources* · large faculty · facilities · opportunity for exposure to content from other professions	*Constituency* · direct access to audience (association members) *Credibility* · official representative of profession *Financing* · non profit status *Resources* · access to wide array of faculty (association members)	*Constituency* · direct access to audience (employees) · opportunity for contact with other professions *Credibility* · opportunity for linkage of education with practice *Financing* · minimum loss of work time for participants *Resources* · scheduling convenience · direct and continuous assessment of performance	*Constituency* · may serve own audience in a new way *Credibility* · freedom to create own image *Financing* · able to amortize costs over many programs *Resources* · marketing expertise · innovative formats and methods · quick response to learners' needs because CPE is primary function
Constraints	*Constituency* · no natural audience (except alumni) *Credibility* · inability to link education with practice *Financing* · unreliable funding because CPE is not primary function *Resources* · limited incentives for faculty participation	*Constituency* · limited contact with other professions *Credibility* · decision-making structure leads to lack of long-term leadership in CPE *Financing* · unreliable funding because CPE is not primary function *Resources* · limited facilities · limited staff devoted to education	*Constituency* · work concerns may interfere with full attention to education *Credibility* · limited vision of solving problems through education *Financing* · unreliable funding because CPE is not primary function · relatively higher cost for education *Resources* · lack of high-level educational leadership	*Constituency* · may not have a natural audience *Credibility* · not primary source of research and theory · low image of educational quality *Financing* · sensitive to general economy *Resources* · limited facilities

The Institutional Context of Effective Practice

One primary goal of people working in institutions is to do what they do well, whether it is producing automobiles, offering health care, or providing education. If an organization is working well, all of its subunits will be working together toward the same ends. The educational subunit is part of this larger institutional context, and helps to determine the way its members go about their work. Continuing professional educators are not independent agents serving their audience in ways that only they believe is appropriate. Rather, their concept of which audience to serve and how to serve it is conditioned by the demands of the parent institution as it tries to survive and prosper. Continuing professional educators must constantly be sensitive to how their effort relates to basic organizational goals.

Continuing professional educators practice in different types of institutional contexts and have different educational functions. Thus, effectiveness is judged in different ways. Some organizations use continuing education as a means of improving the performance of professionals, others use it to generate income, and still others use it as a public relations strategy. Some of these functions are not ideal and may contradict an educator's vision about the true purpose of continuing professional education. Yet these functions are powerful determinants of effective practice. If continuing professional educators are to survive and prosper, they must keep in mind the educational goals institutionally defined as effective.

The key question is: What is the relationship of the continuing education unit to the basic purposes of the agency of which it is a part? A broad classification scheme has been used to analyze the different forms that these relationships can take in other adult education agencies (Darkenwald and Merriam, 1982). Fundamental differences flow from these relationships regarding the audience (or market) and the mission of a continuing education unit. No matter what type of agency continuing educators work in, the key leadership challenge is to position "continuing education activities so that they come to be seen as actively contributing to the attainment of institutional goals" (Simerly, 1987, p. 214).

Relationship to the Parent Agency

Darkenwald and Merriam (1982, p. 155) propose that adult educational agencies relate to the purposes of their parent organization in four different ways. Based on this scheme, continuing professional education can be the primary function of an agency, a secondary function of an educational agency, a complementary function of a quasi-educational agency, or a supportive function of a noneducational agency. The four major types of continuing professional education providers correspond fairly well to these four orientations. However, the boundaries between orientations are somewhat blurred and there is some difficulty in classifying all institutions into one orientation or another. In the following section, these orientations are arrayed on a continuum, beginning with the one in which continuing education is the most derivative of the parent's basic operating goals, and proceeding to the one in which it is central to the agency's basic purpose.

Noneducational organizations use continuing education to enhance the achievement of their fundamental mission. For example, the basic purpose of schools is to teach children, of architectural firms to design buildings, and of hospitals to restore patients to health. In these types of settings, continuing education is more a means than an end to its parent institution's goals.

Earlier in this chapter, employing agencies were characterized as using education as a means of improving their primary service or product. In these settings, professionals' needs are usually of less concern than organizational needs in determining the content of continuing education programs. For example, the administrators of a hospital felt a need to help patients leave more quickly after surgery because its third-party payers would only reimburse a patient's stay for a specified number of days. Thus, the continuing education unit implemented a program to teach nurses some physical therapy strategies that could be used with patients to promote a quicker recovery.

Continuing educators in employing agency settings usually need to demonstrate how their efforts relate to effectively providing the parent's basic service or product.

Professional associations are an example of *quasi-educational organizations* in that continuing education is only one of their basic purposes. Associations are organized to advance the interests of their members. Most are devoted to their members' professional development, as well as to legislative lobbying, maintaining certification programs, and promoting the public image of the profession. Associations vary in the importance they attach to education. Some consider continuing education one of their most important responsibilities and have a full-time educational director. Other associations attach little importance to education and thus have no one to handle it.

Continuing professional education is a *secondary function* of universities and professional schools in which preparatory education is a primary function. In this position the heads of continuing education units are usually at a disadvantage in fighting for institutional resources. This is often true even for those units that have a long history, large staffs, and sizable budgets. Continuing education units are marginal, and will continue to be so until the higher education faculty considers the instruction of practicing professionals a mainstream responsibility (Toombs, Lindsay, and Hettinger, 1985; Vicere, 1985).

Independent providers have two orientations to continuing education. Agencies such as pharmaceutical companies that use continuing professional education to market their products or services are noneducational providers. They use continuing education as a way to achieve another organizational end. In contrast, the business of selling continuing professional education programs is a primary function of the "private" providers, so the mission of the parent body and the continuing education unit is the same. Continuing educators in these agencies have a great deal of discretion in what they do because their work does not derive from the operating goals of a parent body.

Market Relationships

The relationship of the continuing education unit to its parent body has important implications for how its market is defined. Moving on a continuum from noneducational to independent agencies, the audience or market for continuing education becomes increasingly external. The audience for continuing education in employing agencies, their employees, is almost completely internal. There is little need to market these programs to professionals outside the organization. Some units do this only as a secondary activity to the education of the employees. Professional associations also have a constituency, their members and others in the profession who are not members. Association members have some affinity and allegiance to the programs of the association. However, the association has little formal control over its members and so must market these programs to them. Universities and independent providers share a similar situation, in that they do not have a constituency for their programs. Thus, the market for both of these providers is totally external. The only part of the market that has some natural affinity to universities and professional schools is their own graduates. Independent providers generally have to start from scratch in building up a constituency.

At least three types of providers serve external audiences that have varying degrees of allegiance to them. Azzaretto (1987) suggests that continuing educators must develop a competitive strategy in order to secure a sufficient number of participants from these audiences. He offers five components of a competitive planning model for continuing professional education providers.

The first is that the provider must have an internal orientation to service excellence. First popularized by Peters and Waterman (1982), the "customer-driven" organization is now seen as a key in any people-intensive business such as continuing professional education. Second, providers must attend to the processes of market segmentation and positioning. Taken together, these two concepts provide a basis for developing instructional programs that meet client needs, are market competitive, and are based on what the provider does best. The third element is to develop a focused operating and geographic strategy. That is, providers should be clear about why and where they are serving their audience. The fourth part of the strategy is to establish partnerships and coalitions, a topic that is treated at length in the next chapter. Fifth, the ultimate test for a competitive strategy is that participants perceive the quality and cost effectiveness of the educational product as high.

Taken together, these elements make up an organized plan to analyze a provider's existing strengths and resources. By using this plan to design and deliver programs, continuing educators can increase the likelihood of developing effective market relationships.

Educational Mission and Effective Practice

The institutional context strongly influences the focus of continuing professional educators' practice. This occurs because the purposes of the parent agency determine to a great extent the mission of the continuing education unit or function. Continuing educators themselves can help shape the mission and operating agenda for their unit, and a number of strategies are available for them to do so (Knox, 1981; Simerly and Associates, 1987; Votruba, 1981). Instead of slavishly carrying out the ends of their parent organization, they can work within a discretionary framework set up by the goals and resources of the parent agency. For example, the director of education in a professional association may be able to increase the importance of the educational function within her work setting, although she will probably never convince the association that it should test member performance as a basis for developing continuing education programs. Regardless of the amount of discretion continuing educators have in defining their mission, the effectiveness of their practice cannot be determined independent of the institutional context in which it occurs. Ultimately, whether institutional goals are served is the major criterion of the value of any educational practices.

▼

CHAPTER 6

Deciding When to Collaborate with Other Educational Providers

THE APPROACHES TO interorganizational relationships in continuing professional education have often been identified as a choice between competition and collaboration (Cervero, 1984; Houle, 1980; Smutz, Crowe, and Lindsay, 1986). For example, Hazzard (1977) asked the question of continuing education in science and engineering: "Is it best just to let the free market operate with supply responding to demand in the many ways already extant? Or should there be more bureaucratic ways of response?" (p. 190). Some observers conclude that the formation of collaborative relationships among providers is most desirable (National University Continuing Education Association, 1984). Others proclaim that competition can produce higher quality education (Bloom, 1983; Kost, 1980; Griffith, 1983). Their argument is: "Let the various providers do what seems best and the test of the marketplace will prevail" (Houle, 1980, p. 194).

Decision making regarding interorganizational relationships has become an important component of effective practice in continuing professional education. For example, in a case study (Cervero, 1984b) of a large university-based continuing professional education office, the director said that over half of his staff members have doctorates in continuing education and are quite capable of planning programs on their own. Yet, forming relationships with other providers is a key strategy in his agency's immediate and long-term program development efforts. This director's orientation is not unique. Many, if not most, continuing professional education agencies find it desirable to form relationships with other providers.

One reason for the prominence of interorganizational relationships in continuing education is that they are also used extensively at the preservice level of professional education. Thus, it is natural that continuing educators look to the many models and examples in their own experience based on preservice professional training. Two examples from medical education are illustrative. First, professional schools and community hospitals have had formal collaborative arrangements to provide clinical experience for interns and residents for many years. Second, professional specialty associations virtually dictate the content of the professional school curriculum in their specialties because they control the certification examinations.

This chapter describes a typology of strategies that providers use in relating to external institutions for the purpose of developing educational activities. Following this is a discussion of the extent to which these strategies are used and the arguments that commonly promote different strategies. Then, a framework is outlined that can be used to understand why decision makers use these various strategies.

A Typology of Interorganizational Relationships

One of the problems that plagues discussions about the formation of relationships among providers is the lack of clarity about the phenomenon being discussed. Nowhere is a definition of competition among providers given, although many people appear to assume it means the absence of cooperation. The presence of a relationship among providers has been described by such terms as cooperation (Beder, 1984a), collaboration (Cervero, 1984), partnership (Nowlen and Stern, 1981), and interdependence (Fingeret, 1984). Schermerhorn (1975) argues that the lowest common denominator among these concepts is organizational interdependence. Litwak and Hylton (1962) consider two or more organizations interdependent if they take each other into account in pursuing individual goals. Thus, a continuum can be conceptualized in which there is a high degree of interdependence at one end and a low degree at the other.

Cervero and Young (1987) have proposed a typology of organizational interdependence among continuing professional education providers that includes six qualitatively different orientations or action strategies. They are monopoly, parallelism, competition, cooperation, coordination, and collaboration. Although finer distinctions may be identified within the six, the typology is intended to include all possible ways that any one provider can relate to other providers. It is not assumed that greater interdependence is a more highly valued or successful action strategy than less interdependence. The orientations are arranged from least to greatest degree of interdependence.

Monopoly. In this orientation, a provider is the only one of its type in a service area, such as a university or a professional association, or is the only one that has programs in a certain content area in a certain location. This kind of situation occurs because of circumstances or tradition, or it can be mandated by an authority such as a board of education. For example, the state may mandate a specific program and contract with a single institution to exclusively provide it. This occurred in Illinois when the Department of Registration and Education had suspended the licenses of a group of physicians for substance abuse. The department required them to participate in a continuing education program sponsored by a specific university to address this problem before renewing their licenses. In this orientation a provider does not need to take any other provider into account in planning a continuing education program.

Parallelism. Cross (1981) suggests that continuing education providers

> can run parallel operations. In the beginning, the relationship between collegiate institutions and other providers of education services was essentially parallel. . . . Each went along its well-defined paths. Many educators still act as though parallelism still predominates. Plodding along their own

> paths, they pretty much keep to themselves, quite
> unaware of travelers on other pathways [p. 2].

Occasionally, a provider finds that others are offering the same kinds of programs, but usually continues on the assumption that the market is large enough for more than one provider. For example, all four types of providers may be offering a program about AIDS to health professionals at about the same time in a major metropolitan area. In this strategy there is almost no interdependence and what does occur results from chance encounters among providers.

Competition. Many cite competition as a possible action strategy for continuing education providers (Beder, 1984b; Cross, 1981). In this orientation two or more providers offer programs on a specific topic with full knowledge that others are doing the same. This strategy often occurs in management development programming, in which independent consultants, employer training departments, professional associations, university business departments, and continuing education units all offer similar courses (Azzaretto, 1987). Where there is a substantial number of potential participants, no provider will suffer program cancellations or loss of prestige. However, where there is a limited number of participants, conflict among the providers can result. While the providers are not working together to achieve mutual goals, the acts of one can obviously affect the others in an immediate way.

Cooperation. Cooperation refers to the strategy in which providers assist each other on an ad hoc basis (Whetten, 1981). For example, an association may sell its membership list to a seminar business, or a university may recommend several of its faculty for a program being developed by a CPA firm. In so doing, the two providers become interdependent, albeit on a limited basis. Although cooperation appears to be a common form of interaction among continuing professional education providers, its incidence has not been systematically researched.

Coordination. In this orientation providers ensure that their activities take into account those of others on a consistent basis (Lindsay, Queeney, and Smutz, 1981). The coordination of educational services can occur by mandate from a higher authority, by interorganizational agreements, or by what Cross (1981) defines as a second form of parallelism:

> It is the model in which each provider performs a unique function within well-defined boundaries. . . . In the jargon of the trade, this is known as seeking the "market niche," which means simply that providers who are potentially competitive will seek the unique service where competition is weak or non-existent. . . . Parallelism can be maintained only through conscious and sustained effort and by careful definition of non-overlapping functions [p. 3].

For example, a corporation such as IBM may sponsor a program in a specific technical area that is not covered in typical graduate curricula.

A different kind of coordination occurs when two universities agree to program in noncompeting content areas, such as electrical and mechanical engineering. In this case each provider would seek to develop programs in the area in which their faculty is the most prominent. This strategy requires a high degree of interdependence among providers. The major difference between this orientation and collaboration is that in the latter the providers work together on a single program.

Collaboration. Collaboration refers to providers "working together jointly and continuously on a particular project towards a specific goal" (Lindsay, Queeney, and Smutz, 1981, p. 5). When most people think of high degrees of interdependence this is the form of interaction they usually have in mind. The most common example of collaboration is cosponsorship of a program by two or more providers. For example, a professional association, state department of energy, and university engineering department might cosponsor a program on nuclear plant construction for engineers. There is a great deal of variation in the nature of the agreements between providers, depending on their degree of formality and the organizational level at which they are negotiated (Lindsay, Queeney and Smutz, 1981; Marrett, 1971). Collaborations may occur either by informal agreement or legal contract.

Use of Interdependent Strategies

Several studies have used national samples to study the extent to which providers form collaborative relationships with one another (Knox, 1982; Nowlen and Stern, 1981; Younghouse and Young, 1984). The literature also describes hundreds of examples of particular collaborations. But except for scattered anecdotal reports, no research has been undertaken that answers the question of how much programming is done on a collaborative versus a competitive basis. One exception to this is that Cervero (1984b) found that the continuing education programming unit at the University of Illinois cosponsors 70 percent of its programs with other organizations. Although this figure may be high when compared with other providers, both national surveys and institutional descriptions suggest that highly interdependent relationships are formed with much greater frequency than the nondata-based literature indicates.

A national study of all accredited medical schools in the United States found that approximately 70 percent cosponsor ongoing continuing medical education programs with community hospitals (Younghouse and Young, 1984). As reported by continuing education deans and directors, some of the consequences of these collaborative arrangements for medical schools were that they (1) fulfilled part of the medical schools' missions and goals, (2) increased the medical schools' image and visibility, (3) provided visibility to new medical school faculty, and (4) increased referrals to the medical schools' teaching hospitals and clinics.

Knox (1982) conducted a national study of university-based continuing professional education programming units in five fields — medicine, pharmacy, social work, education, and law. He found that while small programs seemed unconcerned about working with other providers, large offices depended on effective relationships with other providers for maintaining the size and diversity of their efforts. They did this by cosponsoring programs that would have had less attendance if they were provided independently. He also found that while these university units collaborated with other types of providers, they tended not to form relationships with other university units:

> In each of the five fields there were many examples of cosponsorship and other forms of collaboration between the office and associations and employers. . . . Most of the CPE offices in medical schools had established relationships with cooperating hospitals, which included provision of CPE, opportunities for internships and residencies for medical students and sources of patient referrals for teaching and research. The most noteworthy examples of collaboration illustrated the importance of mutual benefits. There were few examples of sustained collaboration with other professional schools in the same field, in part illustrating the lack of complementarity on which sustained cooperation usually depends [Knox, 1982, p. 122].

A 1979 study of association/university collaboration efforts included 110 professional associations and 136 universities (Nowlen and Stern, 1981). This study found that 48 percent of the associations and 85 percent of the universities had undertaken collaborative programming. The chief benefits of collaboration for universities were strengthened awareness of university capabilities (88 percent), the collegiality generated (88 percent), improvement in the quality of the association program (85 percent), and that as a result of this experience one or more additional professional groups approached the university to explore cooperation (83 percent). The associations believed that they had benefited more from the relationship financially than had the universities. The associations perceived that their chief benefits were an improved association program (90 percent), a greater awareness of university capabilities (79 percent), improved professional competence (70 percent), and the generation of collegiality between association and university personnel at various levels (70 percent).

This study encountered major problems in these collaborations. Among the association, 48 percent reported "turf" definition problems (who was responsible for what), 25 percent said that university business procedures were inadequate, and 10 percent felt that faculty behaved unprofessionally. Among the universities, 43 percent encountered turf definition problems, 36 percent had difficulty with dorm accommodations, and 26 percent found costs higher than expected.

There is no shortage of descriptions of particular collaborative programs. Several examples come from the fields of teaching (Ferver, 1981; Davies and Aquino, 1975) medicine (Manning and others, 1979), and accounting (Cruse, 1983). Eurich (1985) also provides several examples between universities and employers. Seattle University's School of Engineering, with assistance from Boeing, has started a new master's degree for software engineering to accommodate Boeing's employees as well as other students. Fifteen universities from the Association for Media-Based Continuing Education for Engineers, together with twelve leading corporations, have developed the National Technological University (NTU). This university operates by satellite to reach engineers in corporate classrooms for advanced professional work leading to NTU's master of science degree (Eurich, 1985). Cross (1981) describes four models of university/industry cooperation and gives several examples of each. On a continuum these models range from industry's control over what and how content is taught to higher education's control over these educational functions.

A final example of collaborative programs is the Continuing Professional Education Development Project. The project was begun in 1980 as a five-year research and development effort funded by the W. K. Kellogg Foundation, Pennsylvania State University, and fourteen participating professional associations (Lindsay, Queeney, and Smutz, 1981). A major goal of the project was to establish collaborative relationships between the university and the professional associations for the purpose of strengthening the development and implementation of continuing education programs. Collaboration was implemented by developing a "profession team" for each of the five selected professional groups: accounting, architecture, clinical dietetics, clinical psychology, and gerontological nursing. Each team included representatives from national and state professional associations, regulatory agencies, Pennsylvania State University faculty members from appropriate academic departments, and project staff members. By the completion of the project, programs had been developed collaboratively for each of these professions.

Value of Interdependent Strategies

There appears to be only a small amount of support for encouraging competitive relationships. Almost all those who support competition among providers base their arguments on the free market system of the economy; they believe that only the highest quality (Bloom, 1983; Kost, 1980), best managed (Stern, 1983b), and most effectively delivered (Griffith, 1983) programs survive. Kost (1980) presents the most direct argument for competition when he says: "Competition is needed to drive up the quality of such programs or to replace them in the marketplace. Competition is also needed to produce more innovative approaches in curriculum planning, program development, instruction, and program delivery" (p.42). In a different argument for competition, Curran (1983) believes that professional associations in banking should reduce interdependent relationships with universities because of previous negative experiences in which universities took control of program content and delivery. No one believes that competition should be the only principle governing relationships among providers. Even those who support competition, such as Kost (1980) and Bloom (1983), see the need for competitive and cooperative relationships to coexist.

The relative value of high degrees of interdependence among providers of continuing education has been discussed in the context of many professions, including teaching (Ferver, 1981), engineering (Bruce, Siebert, Smullin, and Fano, 1982), and medicine (Derbyshire, 1983). Although, as has been shown, interdependence is a common mode of operation at the present time, the literature overwhelmingly supports the need for even more interdependence among providers of continuing professional education. The most common way of promoting interdependence is to advocate its desirability without being specific about the ends it serves or the form it should take (Berlin, 1983; National University Continuing Education Association, 1984; Ryor, Shanker, and Sandefeur, 1979; Stern, 1980). Berlin (1983) provides some insight to support interdependent relationships as a general good: "Cooperative or collaborative arrangements have a beguiling appeal, sustained at least in part by the rhetoric of the idea and its apparent political correctness" (p. 127).

Others are more specific about the form interdependence should take. Several authors propose developing a superordinate body to coordinate continuing education in the professions. Eurich (1985) proposes a "strategic council for educational development" to coordinate the programs offered by multiple providers. Lynton (1983) suggests forming "human resource councils" to perform this function. Bruce, Siebert, Smullin, and Fano (1982) propose a council that "insures speedy development of lifelong cooperative education by aggressively promoting and supporting collaborative efforts by industry and engineering schools" (p. 46). And several authors have suggested that interdependent relationships are helpful toward achieving a specific end, such as manpower development (Shelton and Craig, 1983), improved performance of practitioners (Houston and Freiberg, 1979), and improved patient care (Derbyshire, 1983).

In discussing the reasons that interdependence among providers should be encouraged, a number of authors have identified the benefits that providers should expect as a result. By collaborating with employers and associations, higher education institutions improve their access to potential students (Lynton, 1981; Smutz, Crowe, and Lindsay, 1986) and their ability to identify learning needs (Smutz, Crowe, and Lindsay, 1986). Professional associations improve their access to faculty, obtain the use of better facilities, and decrease their program development costs by collaborating with institutions of higher education

(Smutz, Crowe, and Lindsay, 1986). Employers can provide education in a more cost-effective manner by buying what they need than by developing and delivering it themselves. Furthermore, they also enhance the regular access of their employees to new knowledge (Lynton, 1981). It is both difficult and expensive for employers to duplicate the structure and service of a tax-supported higher education system. By collaborating with associations and places of higher learning, an independent provider can share their aura of quality as well as their nonprofit privileges for mailings (Suleiman, 1983).

The development of interdependent relationships also has its problems. Efforts to develop relationships between providers are likely to fail if their only basis is the belief that such relationships are good (Eurich, 1985; Lynton, 1981). For most collaborations to be successful they should be concentrated in specific areas that are congenial to the needs and capabilities of both providers.

A number of deterrents to the formation of interdependent relationships between higher education and other providers have been noted. Smutz, Crowe, and Lindsay (1986) explain that there are deep-seated value differences between higher education and other providers. For example, whereas higher education is primarily concerned with individual development in its continuing education endeavors, employers use continuing education primarily to develop their organizations. Employers criticize universities for being too inflexible about the time, place, and format of their offerings. Universities offer continuing education that is both too narrowly focused on the cognitive domain and too theoretical. Employers often complain that universities do not know how to teach adults properly (Lynton, 1981).

Forming Interorganizational Relationships

Much of the discussion and research on the topic of relationships among providers is prescriptive and descriptive. That is, the focus is on the desirability and frequency of use of different interorganizational strategies. It is still not clearly understood why providers find it necessary or desirable to work with each other. Practice is most effective when it proceeds from a clear understanding of why educators choose to engage in certain actions and not in others. Interagency collaboration could be more effectively stimulated or facilitated if a knowledge base provided insight into why decision makers engage in such relationships.

What is presented here is a framework that describes the conditions under which continuing professional education providers choose to form different types of interorganizational relationships. (An earlier version of this framework is published elsewhere [Cervero and Young, 1987].) The fundamental assumption in developing the framework is that providers *decide* to engage in interdependent relationships with one another (Schermerhorn, 1975). Individuals make their decisions about forming interorganizational relationships under constraints imposed by organizational and environmental conditions. The logic of the framework is that certain motivating conditions cause a decision maker to engage in such strategies as cooperation, coordination, or collaboration. If none of these motivating conditions exists, the decision maker is likely to use one of the other strategies — monopoly, parallelism, or competition — in relating to other providers.

Three conditions are described in the following sections that motivate decision makers to view high degrees of interdependence as a possible organizational strategy. Once these motivating conditions exist, decision makers find themselves in a cost-benefit dynamic wherein the need for interdependent relationships is balanced against (1) the costs of entering such relationships and (2) the actual possibilities presented to them within their specific organizational and environmental context. If the benefits exceed the costs, interdependent relationships become a preferred action strategy that the decision maker seeks to implement in developing a special educational program.

Motivators. The motivating conditions influencing interorganizational interdependence derive from the benefits potentially associated with such activities. Schermerhorn (1975) has identified three important motivators.

1. Providers will seek out or be receptive to interorganizational cooperation when faced with situations of resource scarcity or performance distress (Schermerhorn, 1975, p. 848). This is well supported in the general organizational literature (Mulford, 1984), and is consistent with practice and research in continuing education (Lindsay, Queeney, and Smutz, 1981). Schermerhorn suggests that providers may be favorably predisposed toward cooperative relationships when there is a need to (a) gain access to otherwise unavailable resources, (b) free internal resources for alternative uses, or (c) use existing resources more efficiently. These conditions often motivate universities, for example, to seek cosponsorship arrangements with employing institutions such as schools, hospitals, or social service agencies. These institutions can deliver a regular flow of participants as well as information about their needs, thereby eliminating the necessity for the university to expend human and financial resources on marketing and needs assessment.

2. Providers will seek out or be receptive to interorganizational cooperation when cooperation per se takes on a positive value (Schermerhorn, 1975, p. 848). This positive valuing may arise from internal organizational conditions or from norms in the external environment. As established earlier in this chapter, many providers generally feel that cooperation with others is intrinsically good. As a result many providers are receptive to or actively seek out relationships simply because it seems to be the right thing to do. This is the factor that Beder (1984b) terms "goal orientation" and that was found by Cervero (1984b) and Fingeret (1984) to influence the extent of interdependence among continuing professional education providers.

3. Providers will seek out or be receptive to interorganizational cooperation when a powerful extra-organizational force demands this activity (Schermerhorn, 1975, p. 849). Such demands may stem from government or third-party organizations such as insurance companies. Fingeret (1984) found this to be a powerful motivator when the Nuclear Regulatory Commission forced utility companies to cooperate with universities in training their engineering employees.

Costs. Once decision makers are motivated to consider the possibility of forming interorganizational relationships, they begin to identify costs that might potentially be associated with cooperative activities. Three major ones are reviewed below.

1. Participation in interorganizational cooperation may involve a loss of decision-making autonomy (Schermerhorn, 1975, p. 849). This is particularly true for the strategies of cooperation and collaboration, where obligations, commitments, or contracts with other providers place constraints on each provider. Because there is a commitment for joint decision making about future activities, limits are placed on unilateral decisions. This can become a severe problem when one partner makes demands that the other does not agree with for such things as location, cost, or content of the program being developed.
2. Participation in interorganizational cooperation may involve unfavorable ramifications for organizational image or identity (Schermerhorn, 1975, p. 849). Cooperative activities with certain organizations may adversely affect a provider's prestige, identity, or strategic position in the marketplace. The clearest example is the reluctance of many universities and professional associations to form relationships with independent for-profit providers. By cooperating with the for-profit sector, many decision makers in these institutions believe they tarnish their image of credibility. At the same time they damage their strategic position in the market by lending credence to the for-profit providers' future programming efforts. In its subsequent marketing efforts, the for-profit provider will probably list the university or association as a previous cooperating partner.
3. Participation in interorganizational cooperation may involve costs by requiring the direct expenditure of scarce organizational resources (Schermerhorn, 1975, p. 850). In most cases, it takes more time and energy to develop and implement a cosponsored program than to develop the same program alone. In addition to the time required for meetings to develop the program, there are actual direct expenditures such as for transportation and communication activities.

Many providers may simply not have the resources to invest in such cooperative ventures. Knox (1982) found that the large continuing education offices in universities are much more likely to engage in cooperative activities than are small offices because they have more resources to invest in cooperative activities.

Organizational and Environmental Determinants. A balancing set of factors that decision makers must consider is the organizational and environmental capacities to support cooperative endeavors. Three primary ones are described below.

1. To the extent that providers' boundaries are open and permeable vis-à-vis the external environment, they are more likely to employ interorganizational cooperation as a strategy (Schermerhorn, 1975, p. 850). The Pennsylvania State project (Smutz and Toombs, 1985) provides strong evidence for this proposition in its study of boundary spanners. These are individuals who cross their organizations' boundaries to link with other organizations in the environment. The researchers found that of the two types of providers in the project, domain-protecting ones were much less likely than domain-expanding ones to seek cooperative relationships. Thus, each type of provider strategically selected boundary spanners who were most likely to support their orientation. In working with the other organizations in the project, domain-protecting providers used individuals with low-level positions in the organization, whereas domain-expanding providers selected individuals who were influential within their own organization (Smutz and Toombs, 1985).
2. When two or more providers experience and recognize some mutual need or purpose, and organizational domains are not sensitive issues, they are more likely to employ interorganizational cooperation as a strategy (Schermerhorn, 1975, p. 851). For this to occur, two conditions need to be met. The providers' domains or official goals must be complementary rather than similar. Schermerhorn (1975) explains: "Since official goals relate an organization to specific input and output domains, goal similarity at this level might well imply

competition as opposed to cooperation" (p. 851). As an example of this principle, Cervero (1984b) and Knox (1982) both found that universities generally do not collaborate with each other, even when they have extensive relationships with other types of providers. Schermerhorn (1975) continues: "Given that domains are not a sensitive issue, however, divergent operating goals would seem to offer little basis for cooperative relations. Thus, interorganizational cooperation appears more likely in situations where organizational domains are not sensitive issues (complementary official goals) and where mutual performance objectives are perceived (common operative goals)" (p. 851). For cooperative activities to flourish, both providers must benefit. The key to the perception of mutual need lies in a reciprocal relationship in which both partners exchange resources that are valued less for resources that are valued more (Beder, 1984c).

3. To the extent that interorganizational cooperative activity can be supported by sufficient resources providers are likely to use interorganizational cooperation as a strategy (Schermerhorn, 1975, p. 852). The geographical proximity of potential partners was found by Cervero (1984b) and Beder (1984c) to be an important correlate of cooperation among continuing education providers. An important determinant at the interorganizational level is a provider's internal capacity to build and support cooperative activities. Schermerhorn suggests that the relevant factors for this determinant include a provider's existing level of cooperative activity, the availability of slack resources to build and explore cooperative ventures, and the ability to mobilize these resources for application to interorganizational cooperation. For example, if a professional association has only one person managing the educational unit, this individual may only have time to perform the basic functions of developing a yearly conference, with no other time available for long-term program development efforts.

Cost-Benefit Dynamic. The framework's fundamental proposition is that while motivators are necessary, they are not sufficient stimuli to engage in highly interdependent relationships. A complex decision-making process occurs regarding the potential costs or a lack of organizational and environmental capacities, the provider might see the possibility of forming highly interdependdiscussion within an organization. These decisions are made in three ways. First, if none of the three motivating conditions are present, a decision maker would have no interest in forming highly interdependent relationships. Thus, the provider would most likely engage in the strategies of monopoly, parallelism, or competition. Second, if at least one of the motivating conditions is present but the decision maker perceives high potential costs or a lack of organizational and environmental capacities, the provider might see the possibility of forming highly interdependent relationships but would not receive that extra push to view them as a preferred action strategy. So the decision maker would still most likely engage in monopoly, parallelism, or competitive strategies. Third, with the presence of at least one motivator, a low risk of incurring costs, and sufficient organizational and environmental capacities, the provider would seek out or be receptive to highly interdependent relationships. This provider would be likely to engage in the strategies of cooperation, coordination, or collaboration. As more motivators, fewer costs, and greater organizational and environmental capacities are present, the likelihood of entering highly interdependent relationships increases.

A Concluding Note

Should interorganizational relationships be promoted as a general strategy in continuing professional education? The answer is that highly interdependent relationships will be developed according to the outcomes of the decision-making dynamic, not simply perceived "political correctness." It seems unreasonable to argue that collaborative relationships should be promoted as a general strategy. There is as yet no evidence that such relationships work any better than competitive relationships in producing more desirable outcomes, such as higher-quality, more accessible, or more effective continuing education. The view expressed by others (Beder, 1984b; Eurich, 1985; Lynton, 1981) that highly interdependent relationships do not necessarily produce the best programs is the most defensible at the present time. The formation of these relationships is simply a means to an end. Only when ends are defined and the effectiveness of interdependent relationships is established will it be possible to establish whether greater degrees of interdependence are worth promoting as a general strategy in continuing professional education.

▼

CHAPTER 7

Successful Program Development Strategies

WE ARE FACED WITH a great irony when approaching the topic of how best to develop programs for professionals. Precious little research documents how competent educators actually develop programs and what distinguishes the program development processes of successful and unsuccessful continuing educators. Yet this is the area in which the greatest number of people working in continuing professional education are involved. Everyone, from the tens of thousands of instructors to the deans of professional schools and vice-presidents for education in associations and employing agencies, has a responsibility to develop programs for his or her respective constituency.

Although a solid research base is lacking, there is no shortage of books and articles that prescribe how program development ought to occur. Literally dozens of planning frameworks claim to be relevant to specific professions and a handful claim to be useful for all professions. These prescriptive textbook frameworks are generally treated with a great deal of skepticism, at least from those with "years of experience dealing with organizations in which personality conflicts, political factors, and budgetary constraints constantly alter neatly conceived plans of actions" (Brookfield, 1986, p. 202). This should not be surprising. The little research that has been done suggests that virtually no continuing educators use these planning frameworks, even for programs that are successful.

This does not mean that successful continuing educators do not think about and carry out their work in systematic ways, but simply that textbook planning frameworks do not adequately describe those systematic processes. All continuing educators operate out of their own planning framework, which is influenced by their personal values and beliefs and the institutional context in which they work. The central task for effective practice is to make one's own framework explicit, analyze its assumptions and principles, and alter it when necessary. If continuing professional educators are to become reflective practitioners (Schön, 1983), they must constantly be engaged in this important task.

The purpose of this chapter is to provide some assistance in the difficult endeavor of understanding one's own planning framework. First, some background and a review of textbook frameworks are provided as a context for how to use them. Second, the frameworks for individual professions are analyzed and a more detailed treatment is presented of four frameworks that prescribe program development processes for all professions. Then, program development processes are interpreted in the larger context of professional practice. Continuing educators plan many types of activities, including formal educational programs, self-assessment exercises, skills training in a tutorial setting, and peer review meetings. The term *program,* used in this chapter and the following one on evaluation, should be interpreted to mean any of the forms of educative activity described in Chapter Four.

Which Program Development Framework Should Practitioners Use?

Continuing educators have been planning programs for groups of professionals for decades. These educators have tended to use systematic processes in their planning. In the past twenty years some of these systematic processes have been codified as planning frameworks to provide guidance to others working in the field. Sork and Busky (1986) define a program development framework in a way that is appropriate for this chapter; it is "a set of steps, tasks, or decisions which, when carried out, produce the design and outcome specifications for a systematic instructional activity" (p. 87).

Many people have noted the remarkable similarity of these frameworks to each other in the general field of adult and continuing education (Apps, 1985; Brookfield, 1986; Sork and Busky, 1986) and in continuing professional education (Day and Baskett, 1982; Pennington and Green, 1976). The parentage of nearly all textbook planning frameworks can be traced to Ralph Tyler's (1949) influential book, *Basic Principles of Curriculum Instruction.* Tyler (p. 1) suggests that any curriculum development process should be guided by four questions: (1) What educational experiences should the school seek to attain? (2) What educational experiences can be provided that are likely to attain these purposes? (3) How can these educational purposes be effectively organized? (4) How can we determine whether these purposes are being attained? Apps (1985, pp. 180–181) notes that these four questions can be translated into five tasks common to most program development frameworks: (1) identifying learners' needs, (2) defining objectives, (3) identifying learning experiences that meet these objectives, (4) organizing learning experiences into an educational plan, and (5) evaluating the outcomes of the educational effort in accordance with the objectives.

Most, though not all, authors imply (or state explicitly) that by using their framework one can become a competent continuing educator. These frameworks are prescribed in graduate programs of adult and continuing education and in other forms of professional preparation, such as conferences, seminars, and in-service workshops. However, many successful continuing educators are successful in their work without following these frameworks. The one empirical study of what successful program developers actually do supports the contention that textbook planning frameworks are rarely used, at least by university-based continuing educators. Pennington and Green (1976) interviewed fifty-two continuing professional educators in higher education institutions and asked them to report on the planning processes they used in a recent successful program. In comparing these planning processes with ideal frameworks described in the literature, they found four major discrepancies. First, little comprehensive needs assessment was done due to a lack of time, expertise, or resources. Although most planners gave lip-service to the importance of needs assessment, very few followed through. Second, there was little evidence that available sources were tapped to determine the program's objectives. Objectives were generally not stated in terms of what the learner was supposed to gain from the program. Third, there was no indication that the design of instruction was based on learner characteristics, desired learning outcomes, time, money, or other available resources. After the program was given, comprehensive evaluations were simply not done.

The authors conclude from the way planners described their actions "that personal values, environmental constraints, available resource alternatives, and other factors impinge on the program development process" (Pennington and Green, 1976, p. 22). Houle (1980, p. 228) suggests that this should be seen as positive, not negative, if it means that planners respond to the situation in which they work. The major problem with most textbook planning frameworks is that they are offered in a context-free manner (Brookfield, 1986; Day and Baskett, 1982). Although this may be necessary, Brookfield notes that more authors should "take the time to counsel against the assumption that such models are easily transferable from setting to setting or that a fully supportive economic and political climate will always exist for their implementation" (1986, p. 225).

Effective practice is based on being able to fully understand one's own planning framework, know how to evaluate it, and be able to change it when necessary. Effective practice will not be attained by blindly following someone else's framework. Individual beliefs about learning and education are too diverse and institutional contexts too complex to permit any single framework to be universally appropriate. However, textbook frameworks can be useful as long as continuing educators are aware of their limitations. They should be seen as another source by which to analyze continuing educators' program development practices and thereby understand why these practices are or are not working. They should not be used as prescriptive guidelines to be followed in lockstep fashion. Ultimately "every planner of a continuing education program . . . must remain in control of whatever process, principle, or pattern he or she finds useful" (Houle, 1980, p. 235).

An Overview of Program
Development Frameworks

In Chapter One it was noted that members of a specific profession were at once like no other adults, like some other adults, and like all other adults. Thus, the research, theory, and practice from three sources could be consulted in thinking about their continuing education. This typology is a useful way of organizing the program development frameworks in continuing professional education. First, numerous frameworks prescribe program development processes for a specific profession. Second, four frameworks appear to offer program development guidance across the professions. Third, many frameworks in the literature of adult and continuing education can be helpful in working with all the professions (Houle, 1972; Knowles, 1980; Knox and Associates, 1980). Only the first two types of frameworks are discussed in the sections that follow. The third category is too broad to cover here and the language and examples used in the first two categories are more directly applicable to the topic of this book.

Sork and Busky (1986) have completed a descriptive and evaluative analysis of the program planning literature in the general field of adult and continuing education. As a subset of that review, Sork (1983) has separately analyzed those planning frameworks that focus on continuing professional education. His analysis is used as a basis for an overview of frameworks from individual professions. Although a number of frameworks have been published since Sork's review (for example, Green and others, 1984; Gonnella and Zeleznik, 1983), they do not offer any substantially different insights. Emphasis is placed on the four comprehensive planning frameworks because of the comparative approach to continuing professional education that is used in this book. Sork uncovered one of these frameworks in his review (Pennington and Green, 1976); the other three are of more recent vintage (Houle, 1980; Nowlen, 1988; Queeney and Smutz, forthcoming).

Frameworks from Individual Professions

Sork (1983) found twenty-two reports dealing with program development in continuing professional education, all of which had been published since 1970. Ten of these are books (see Table 3) and the remaining twelve are articles or monograph-length treatments (see Table 4) of planning frameworks. He compared the planning frameworks on six different dimensions. Three dimensions relate to the characteristics of the planning milieu in which they were designed to be used and differ in the level of program emphasized and the client system orientation. The other three are evaluative dimensions that differentiate the frameworks based on features that might limit or enhance their utility for specific users.

Sork made several general observations about planning frameworks in continuing professional education. First, about equal emphasis is given to both the activity levels and organizational levels of programming. Some frameworks emphasize the design of individual educational activities, such as courses or seminars, while others focus on the composite of educational activities provided by a single organization, such as a university or seminar business. Second, most planning frameworks were designed to be used in settings where the potential participants are members of a single formal organization, such as a professional association or employing agency. Only a small number of frameworks were designed for use with general audiences. This characteristic implies the ease with which participants can be identified, which has implications for needs assessments. Third, the level of sophistication needed to use the frameworks is relatively low. Most authors assume that users have little or no training or experience in planning educational programs. Fourth, most of the publications emphasize the "how" rather than the "why" of program development. That is, most authors present a how-to-do-it, cookbook-like framework rather than describing the theoretical assumptions about factors such as how professionals learn. Fifth, the planning steps given the greatest attention are needs assessment, developing objectives, selecting and ordering

Table 3. Analytical Summary of Program Planning Models (Book-Length Publications).

MODEL[a]	DESCRIPTIVE DIMENSIONS						EVALUATIVE DIMENSIONS										
		Level of "Program" Emphasized			Client System Orientation				COMPREHENSIVENESS OF EACH STEP IN THE PLANNING PROCESS								
	Planning Context	Activity	Organizational	Community	Membership	Non-membership	Sophistication Necessary to Benefit or Use Effectively	Degree to Which Model Has Explicit Theoretical Framework	Analyze Context & Client	Assess System Needs	Develop Objectives	Select/Order Content	Select/Order Processes	Select Instr. Resources	Dev. Budget & Admin. Plan	Assure Participation	Design Eval. Procedure
Cooper & Hornback, 1973	CEP	X	X		X		○	◑	⊗	○	○	◑	◑	○	○	○	○
Hospital . . . , 1970	CEP		X		X		◑	○	○	◑	◑	●	○	⊗	○	○	○
Kasaba & Abato, 1971	CEP		X		X		●	○	◑	◑	⊗	⊗	⊗	⊗	⊗	⊗	⊗
Kirk, 1981	CEP	X			X	X	○	⊗	⊗	○	○	○	◑	⊗	⊗	⊗	◑
Lauffer, 1978	CEP	X	X		X		○	⊗	◑	○	○	◑	○	●	◑	◑	⊗
Lauffer, 1977	CEP	X	X		X		○	⊗	○	○	○	○	⊗	◑	○	○	◑
Popiel, 1977	CEP	X	X		X		○	○	○	○	○	○	○	○	○	○	◑
Staropoli & Waltz, 1978	CEP	X			X		◑	○	○	◑	◑	◑	◑	⊗	⊗	●	○
Stearns & Others, 1971	CEP		X		X		◑	○	○	●	○	○	○	⊗	⊗	⊗	○
Tobin & Others, 1979	CEP	X	X		X		○	◑	○	◑	○	◑	◑	◑	○	○	◑

Key to Evaluative Dimensions: ⊗ Not present or not addressed   ○ Low   ◑ Medium   ● High

[a]Listed alphabetically by author within "planning context" categories

Source for Tables 3 and 4: Sork, 1983. Reprinted with permission.

Table 4. Analytical Summary of Program Planning Models (Article and Monograph-Length Publications).

MODEL	DESCRIPTIVE DIMENSIONS							EVALUATIVE DIMENSIONS											
	Planning Context	Level of "Program" Emphasized			Client System Orientation		Sophistication Necessary to Benefit or Use Effectively	Degree to Which Model Has Explicit Theoretical Framework	COMPREHENSIVENESS OF EACH STEP IN THE PLANNING PROCESS									
		Activity	Organizational	Community	Membership	Non-membership			ANALYZE CON. TEXT & CLIENT SYSTEM	ASSESS NEEDS	DEVELOP OBJECTIVE	SELECT/ORDER CONTENT	SELECT/ORDER PROCESSES	SELECT INSTR. RESOURCES	DEV. BUDGET & RESOURCES	ADMIN. PLAN ASSURE PARTICIPATION	DESIGN EVAL. PROCEDURE
Bennett, 1979	CEP	X	X		X	X	◑	⊗	⊗	○	○	○	○	○	○	○	○
Brown & Uhl, 1970	CEP	X	X		X		●	○	○	◑	○	○	⊗	⊗	⊗	⊗	○
Charters & Blakely, 1974	CEP		X		X				○	○	⊗	○	○	○	⊗		
Collert, 1976	CEP	X			X		◑	⊗	⊗	○	○	○	○	⊗	⊗	⊗	◑
Dickinson & Verner, 1974	CEP		X		X		○	○	○	○	○	○	○	⊗	⊗	○	○
Ehrmeyer, 1980	CEP	X			X	X	○	○	⊗	○	⊗	⊗	○	○	⊗	⊗	○
Hutchison, 1974	CEP		X		X		○	○	○	○	○	○	⊗	⊗	⊗	⊗	○
Pennington & Green, 1976	CEP	X	X		X	X	◑	⊗	⊗	○	○	○	○	○	⊗	⊗	○
Smith, 1978	CEP	X			X		◑	⊗	○	○	○	○	○	○	○	○	○
Spikes, 1978a	CEP	X	X		X		◑	⊗	○	○	⊗	⊗	○	⊗	⊗	⊗	○
Spikes, 1978b	CEP	X	X		X		◑	⊗	○	○	⊗	⊗	○	⊗	⊗	⊗	○
Walsh, 1981	CEP	X	X		X		◑	○	○	◑	⊗	⊗	○	⊗	⊗	⊗	○

instructional processes, and designing evaluation procedures. Again the influence of the Tylerian approach to curriculum development is apparent.

Sork also noted the highly prescriptive nature of the planning frameworks, with little attention being given to how program development actually occurs in real-world settings. Another fault he found was that the authors uniformly failed to provide readers with alternative means of completing various planning tasks. This is particularly notable because variations in types of providers, such as a university continuing education unit and the staff development unit in an employing agency, are great enough to require different tactical and strategic planning approaches. In comparing these textbook frameworks with those used in other adult education contexts, the most striking difference was in the "emphasis given in CPE to the linkage between the educational program and the expected changes in the outcomes of professional practice" (Sork, 1983, p. 53).

Cross-Professional Frameworks

Of the four planning frameworks that are designed for use across the professions, the one offered by Pennington and Green (1976) is significantly different in two ways. First, the authors developed their framework from a study of how planners for six different professions report having planned successful programs. As such, it is a descriptive rather than a prescriptive framework. Second, while the goal of the other three is to develop programs that directly affect professional performance, this is not the focus of the planning efforts in Pennington and Green's framework.

Pennington and Green's General Model. The fifty-two planners in the study on which this framework is based developed continuing education programs in eleven higher education institutions for six professions: business administration, educational administration, law, teaching, social work, and medicine. Based on interviews with these planners a program planning model was developed for each of the six fields. These six were combined into one general model, which comprises a series of tasks and decisions that cluster around six groups of activities.

In the first cluster, originating the idea, the idea or request for the program came to or from a person on campus, such as a faculty member or continuing education staff member. Several origins for these ideas included formal needs assessments, requests from a client, availability of project monies, legislative mandates, and suggestions from campus faculty. Once received, the idea was clarified in the cluster labeled developing the idea. Most planners engaged in some activity to set boundaries around the idea, gather resource support, and get preliminary commitments to the possible program. This was done in several ways, including an informal test of the idea with practicing professionals, a review of the literature, a market analysis, or a formal needs assessment. After making the decision to do the program, individuals were identified as planners in the third cluster, making a commitment. Some of the decisions in this cluster included selecting an instructor and deciding whether to use an existing course or a new one. In the fourth cluster, developing the program, instructional design was the main concern; objectives were determined, subject matter was developed, materials were accumulated, and recruitment was completed. In teaching the course, cluster five, the learning activity usually occurred as planned, although some flexibility was maintained for needed changes. Cluster six, evaluating the impact, was usually the result of previous planning, and included such activities as determination of what to evaluate, development of the evaluation instruments, and administration of the evaluation.

Pennington and Green describe program development as "a form of administrative decision-making" (1976, p. 20). A planning agent receives some request or idea for a continuing education activity from inside or outside the organization, and checks its viability according to institutional goals. If it seems viable, the planner gathers resources and makes a number of decisions that in the end shape the educational activity. These decisions involve consideration of a number of contextual factors, such as the environment in which the organization is operating and internal and external constraints and resources. This way of developing programs contrasts sharply with the prescriptive models described in the literature. Some of these differences will become apparent with the examination of the three other frameworks.

Houle's Triple-Mode Model. Houle (1980, pp. 230-234) has proposed a planning framework for developing programs that seeks to strengthen professional performance. Perhaps the most unique aspect of this approach is its emphasis that the planning process itself should be part of the educational activity. He envisions a comprehensive educational process in which the three modes of participation — instruction, inquiry, and reinforcement — are used. He stresses that this planning design can be adapted to many situations, from an individual professional planning his or her own learning to a large organization in which many individuals from different professions work. Houle's framework is a synthesis of several models that were originally proposed in the early 1970s by continuing medical educators. There are ten distinct steps in Houle's program planning process.

First, a list of standards of good practice for a particular entity, such as a department of surgery in a hospital, is developed. The first step is "wholly analytical and seeks to discover what is essential to the most effective operation of the entity" (Houle, 1980, p. 231). If these standards already exist on a national level, the professionals employed in the entity should understand them and agree on their applicability to the local situation. Second, the professionals involved set the ideals of what these standards can accomplish. In step 3, these same professionals establish a floor for what these standards can accomplish. Often the staff who will be part of the process of staff improvement will not have been involved in the first three steps. In these cases it is essential to complete step 4, in which all staff are informed about the steps already taken and approve of what has been done. In step 5, data are collected on current staff performance, based on the criteria of good practice identified in step 1. In step 6, these measurements of performance are compared with both the ideal and minimally acceptable standards (steps 2 and 3) to determine where the performance problems may lie. Then efforts are made to determine the causes of the differences between what is and what ought to be.

Up to this point the professionals have been engaged in the participation modes of inquiry and reinforcement. By identifying possible performance problems, they have been learning about their own practice and possibly will have begun to institute changes in their work routines. In most cases, however, Houle notes that concerted programs of change need to be initiated to correct identified performance deficits. It often happens that these programs of change (step 7) involve a process of learning. Thus, the design of a continuing education program in the mode of instruction is inserted into this larger ten-step framework. In step 8, these instructional programs are carried out in a flexible manner. After the program, current performance on the standards from step 1 are again measured and compared with earlier performance to determine if positive change has occurred (step 9). Depending on the results of the evaluation in this step, programs for further action are considered (step 10). Houle notes that this step completes the cycle but resembles the first step in that a new sequence of actions may start again.

This framework is similar to the general approach to program development based on Tyler's work that was covered earlier in the chapter. The first six steps are an elaborated way of identifying learners' needs; the setting of objectives and identifying and organizing learning experiences are done in steps 7 and 8; and evaluating the outcomes of the educational program occurs in steps 9 and 10.

Practice-Audit Model. This planning framework bears a striking resemblance to Houle's triple-mode model, even though the authors (Queeney and Smutz, forthcoming) do not refer to Houle's work. The major similarities are that both frameworks are practice oriented and that similar processes are used in carrying out the framework. Also, both are prescriptive frameworks, unlike Pennington and Green's, which is descriptive. However, the practice-audit model has been used since the late 1970s when it was developed at Pennsylvania State University in its work with the pharmacy profession. The model was implemented with five other professions in the course of the

1980–85 Continuing Professional Education Development Project conducted at Pennsylvania State. The major unique characteristic of this model is that its implementation to date has involved a collaboration between a higher education institution and professional associations.

This planning framework involves a seven-phase process (Smutz and others, 1981; Queeney and Smutz, forthcoming). In phase 1 a profession team of six to ten members was developed with representatives of (a) the relevant academic department in the university, (b) state and national professional associations, and (c) the national regulatory agency. In addition, two continuing education staff members were assigned to each team. Practice descriptions were developed in phase 2. Each description includes three levels: first, domains or broad areas of practice such as "provide direct patient care"; second, responsibilities such as "assess the patient"; and third, tasks or specific actions of daily practice such as "interview the patient." In their work with the five professions, these practice descriptions consist of 3 or 4 major domains, 10 to 15 responsibilities, and 70 to 120 tasks. These descriptions were then validated by asking practitioners the importance of each task in practice and the frequency with which they perform the task. This phase is very similar to step 1 of Houle's model.

In phase 3, performance assessment materials were developed, and acceptable and unacceptable levels of performance were determined. These materials were designed to follow assessment center concepts, and specific exercises were developed to simulate the practice situation. The exercises usually contained at least one live simulation in which an actor portrayed a client with whom the professional would interact. The practice audit session was actually conducted in phase 4. Each session was a day long and involved forty to fifty members of the profession. The purpose of these sessions was to gather group data on the practice descriptions. Many participants viewed these sessions as a learning experience, thus providing some evidence for Houle's argument that the entire planning process ought to be viewed as a learning activity. In phase 5, the participants' performance was compared to the standards that had been developed in phase 3. Where deficiencies were noted, they formed the basis for educational programming. These three phases clearly correspond to steps 2 through 6 in Houle's model.

Continuing education programs were designed in phase 6 and implemented and evaluated in phase 7. The programs were evaluated by means of a questionnaire sent to participants after six months, asking them how they had used the information presented. This is the only major point of departure from Houle's model, in which participants' actual performance is again assessed as it was before attending the program.

Nowlen's Performance Model. The goal of Nowlen's framework is also the improvement of professional performance. Nowlen's concept of performance is slightly more expansive than the other two. While he believes that workplace dynamics are an important determinant of performance, an equally important determinant is the individuals' personal world. Thus, Nowlen sees individuals "but never without the many contexts in which they live, work, and find meaning" (Nowlen, 1988, p. 122). Of equal importance to individual performance is the collective performance of partners, groups, and institutions. In this way Nowlen's framework mirrors Houle's with the emphasis on involving an entire group within a work setting to improve performance using continuing education.

Nowlen does not propose a new planning framework, but instead offers Houle's (1972) fundamental system of eight decision points that has been designed for general use in adult education. In using this framework, "continuing educators will be able to place the familiar cycles of needs analysis, program design, and evaluation within an overarching learning relationship with organizations as well as individuals" (Nowlen, 1988, p. 123). The key to the framework occurs in the first decision point where a possible educational activity is defined. To be most effective in improving performance, Nowlen argues that a continuing education agency must form a "learning relationship" with a culture of practice, such as a hospital, CPA firm, or school. Only by engaging in an ongoing relationship with a practice setting can a continuing educator truly understand what the problems are and how learning activities may correct them.

By engaging in this collaborative form of program development, continuing educators can collectively bring larger frames of reference to bear on their decisions about the ends of their educational programs. In this way, their efforts reflect the critical approach to continuing education described in Chapter Two. This continuing education unit could be any provider, including a university, the training office of an agency, or an independent provider.

In the second decision point a decision is made to proceed. Many performance goals do not need educational interventions for accomplishment. The continuing educator must focus only on those problems for which there is an educational solution. Once this decision has been made, the third decision point, identifying and refining objectives, becomes a relatively straightforward task. In designing a suitable format within this ongoing learning relationship, decision point four, continuing educators have multiple educational strategies at their disposal. In decision point five, fitting the format into larger patterns of life, the continuing education unit is on very solid footing given the great amount of information it has regarding the professionals with whom it is working. The plan is put into effect in decision point six and the results of the educational program are measured and appraised in seven, at a point mutually determined by the organization and the continuing education agency. Finally, in the eighth decision point, the situation is examined in terms of the possibility of a new educational activity and the planning cycle begins again.

Nowlen notes that few university-based continuing educators presently enjoy this type of intensely collaborative relationship with an employing agency. He points out that, in fact, few educators within employing agencies have such a relationship with their own parent organization. Although these learning relationships are difficult to form, they are necessary for the "long-term performance improvement of the continuing education agency, the organization, and their professionals and executives" (Nowlen, 1988, p. 149).

The last three planning frameworks share many of the characteristics of the single-profession models. First, they are highly prescriptive in offering guidance on how to develop programs. They all either imply or state directly that if continuing educators are to be effective, these frameworks ought to guide their practice. To their credit, in both the practice-audit model and the performance model, extensive descriptions of the context in which they are to be applied offer continuing educators a glimpse into the complexities of real-world planning situations. Yet, they are a distant cry from the descriptive framework of Pennington and Green that, in a summary fashion, describes what continuing educators actually do. These prescriptive frameworks can be useful as long as they are not seen as rigid requirements but rather as concepts that can help continuing educators understand and improve their own planning actions.

Like the single-profession frameworks, these four are strongly influenced by Tyler's conceptions of curriculum development. All four envision a fairly linear process of identifying needs, developing objectives, designing an appropriate educational format, and evaluating the activity. This is particularly interesting for the Pennington and Green model, because even though the planner did not apply it with any rigor, a general model did emerge. However, one must wonder, along with Houle, whether the fifty-two planners had imposed "upon the accounts of their own activities some memories of general patterns that had been described to them" (1980, p. 228). As is necessary with efforts to change performance, the Pennsylvania State, Houle, and Nowlen frameworks have highly elaborated front ends where needs are identified. The first six steps of Houle's model, the first five phases of the practice-audit model, and the formation of learning relationships in Nowlen's model all speak to the importance of correctly identifying the performance that needs to be changed.

Program Development as Professional Work

Program development processes or frameworks are often presented and discussed as if they are a tool to be taken off the shelf and applied as a hammer would be. Unlike the hammer, which is used by most people in the same way, program development frameworks conform to the individuality of the person using them and the context in which they are used. A useful way to understand program development, then, is as a form of practice undertaken by professionals, who in this case are continuing educators. If program development is a form of professional practice, we can analyze it within the functionalist and critical frameworks presented in Chapter Two.

Program development frameworks have generally been offered within the functionalist framework. As described earlier, the key assumptions are that practice problems are well formed and that these problems are solved by the application of scientific knowledge. In this concept of practice, there appears to be general agreement that the goal is to help professionals gain new knowledge, attitudes, or skills. This is done by applying a planning process where needs are assessed, objectives identified, instruction organized, and outcomes evaluated. Continuing educators are urged to think of these planning frameworks as forms of scientific knowledge that will improve their practice if they are applied with great rigor. This way of thinking about professional practice is flawed in several key respects, and accordingly an alternative was proposed (the critical viewpoint).

The critical viewpoint offers a more useful way to understand program development. As with other professionals, continuing educators are regularly confronted with situations that are characterized by uniqueness, uncertainty, or value conflict. Thus, they usually must construct the problem from the situation, using the skills of problem-setting. The knowledge used in this activity is not derived from textbooks, where the prescriptive planning frameworks can be found, but from the educators' repertoire of examples, images, understandings, and actions. Another way of saying this is that continuing educators do not use textbook planning frameworks in their daily work. But this should be seen as the norm of professional practice, rather than something deviant about continuing educators.

Given this understanding, it should not be surprising that most practicing continuing educators reject textbook planning frameworks as descriptive of how they actually work. Argyris and Schön (1974) offer a useful way of understanding this discrepancy by distinguishing between professionals' espoused theories of practice and their theories-in-use. Espoused theories are offered when individuals are asked how they would behave in a given circumstance. This is the theory of action to which allegiance is given and that is communicated to others. The theory that actually governs educators' actions is a theory-in-use, which may or may not be compatible with their espoused theory. Argyris and Schön's central point is that you cannot learn what someone's theory-in-use is by simply asking. Rather, it must be constructed from observing actual behavior.

In this sense all program development frameworks are someone's espoused theories. For example, the practice-audit model, the triple-mode model, and the performance model are all espoused theories. While it may not seem that way at first, Pennington and Green's general model is also an espoused theory because it is based on what planners said they did rather than on actually observing their behavior. This probably explains why the general model looks so much like other planning frameworks and why the authors concluded that the planners did not apply it with any rigor. Continuing educators would be wise to follow Argyris and Schön's admonition "to be skeptical of textbook models of exemplary practice, which they feel frequently represent distorted and highly abstract perceptions of the real world of practice" (Brookfield, 1986, p. 244).

In place of these textbook frameworks, Argyris and Schön argue that professionals must develop their "own continuing theory of practice under real-time conditions" (1974, p. 157). Prescriptive frameworks are useful to the extent that they help to do this. Continuing educators should understand their own theories-in-use about developing programs and use them as effectively as possible, ultimately making their espoused theories congruent with their theories-in-use. These theories-in-use are context-specific and depend on a variety of factors. They include personal beliefs and values about learning, the proper place of the professions in society, and whether continuing educators are trained in the content of a profession. Another set of factors derives from the environment in which continuing educators work. As Knox (1979) points out, most programs are developed in an institutional context, which has profound consequences on a planner's theory-in-use. For example, the four different types of providers described in Chapter Five place continuing educators in different contexts of accountability and different relationships with the parent organization. Different institutions offer different opportunities and constraints, all of which impinge on continuing educators' theory-in-use about developing programs.

These are but a few of the contextual factors that affect theory-in-use. Obviously some theories-in-use are more successful than others because some continuing educators meet their goals more successfully than others. Continuing professional education as a field of practice would become more effective if program developers began to see themselves as "practical theorists" (Brookfield, 1986, p. 244). They can do this by analyzing their own practice and peeling back the layers of words that sometimes obscure the meaning of what they do (Apps, 1985, p. 187). By making explicit and disseminating to others their theories-in-use, program developers could present actual planning frameworks as alternatives to the prescriptive frameworks that so dominate our current discussions.

▼

CHAPTER 8

Determining Whether Programs Are Worthwhile

THE STARTING POINT for this chapter is that "all continuing professional education programming undergoes evaluation, at least in the informal sense" (Knox, 1985a, p. 70). The rationale for this position is that determining the worth of a program — the definition of evaluation used here — is such a fundamental human urge that it is done continually at various levels of formality by learners, instructors, and program planners. The issue is not whether programs should be evaluated, but rather to what extent evaluative information should be collected systematically.

The following statement by several leaders in continuing health professions education illustrates a concept of evaluation that many continuing professional educators subscribe to: "The ultimate criterion for judging the effectiveness of a CE provider unit is the extent to which the continuing education activities of the unit contribute to improved health care of the public. Evaluation is a basic function of the CE provider unit to assess its success or failure in meeting that criterion" (Levine, Moore, and Pennington, 1984). The oft-repeated rationale for this belief is that educators need to "prove" that continuing education makes a difference in professional practice and client outcomes. This belief underlies much of the public discussion about evaluation in continuing professional education. It has been repeated so many times by so many people in so many professions that it has taken on the character of a myth.

Since most continuing educators accept this myth, they are faced with a dilemma in their daily work. Many programs are not intended to directly affect such ultimate outcomes as professional performance or client outcomes. Even in evaluating programs that do seek these types of outcomes, educators do not have the resources to conduct a labor-intensive type of evaluation. Furthermore, no one may be asking educators to justify their programs in this way. In most cases, continuing educators administer end-of-program questionnaires to participants and obtain useful information for planning future programs. Still, a nagging doubt persists that their evaluation efforts are inadequate.

This dilemma is resolvable by stripping away the mythical character of the belief that the ideal evaluation is one that assesses a program's impact on professional performance and client outcomes. Most myths, however, contain some aspect of the truth. In this case the truth is that some programs should be evaluated in terms of their impact on performance. However, this is only one of many useful questions that an evaluation can help to answer. Indeed, in most instances it is not the most appropriate question to ask.

The purpose of this chapter is to provide a framework for organizing the numerous types of evaluation questions that can be asked about continuing professional education programs. First, an overview of evaluation in continuing professional education is presented. Next, a framework of seven types of evaluation questions is suggested. Finally, five criteria are described that are generally used when deciding which types of questions should guide an evaluation effort.

Evaluation in Continuing Professional Education

Houle (1980, p. 237) has identified three frames of reference in which evaluation of continuing professional education is undertaken. The first has to do with the measurement of results of formal educational activities, such as courses, workshops, and seminars. The second has to do with the quality of practice resulting from the learning activities in which professionals are engaged, including formal study and the consequences of education at work. Various evaluation strategies included here are peer appraisal, self-assessment programs, and formal staff appraisal. The third, more general frame of reference estimates the level of performance of an entire profession or some significant sector of it. The recent negative evaluations of the teaching profession, and by implication its continuing education systems, are an example of this frame of reference.

Houle has rightly argued that blurring important differences among these frames of reference has impeded clear public discussion and the improvement of evaluation practices. For example, the myth identified earlier is a grafting of the goals of the second and third frames of reference (assessing the performance of individuals and professional groups) onto the evaluation of formal educational programs. The focus of this chapter is on evaluation as defined in the first of Houle's frames of reference (the results of educative activities), because these are the evaluation activities with which continuing professional educators are centrally concerned. While they may use the results of the evaluations made in the other two frames of reference, continuing educators usually have a limited role in their design and implementation.

Evaluation as the result of educative activity is intimately intertwined with the processes of program development. All of the program development frameworks discussed in the previous chapter have evaluation components built into them. To be effective, evaluation processes must be embedded in the cycle of program development. The primary reason for discussing evaluation separately is that it has taken on enormous significance in continuing professional education. However, this discussion should be viewed in the context of the program development frameworks analyzed in the previous chapter.

The evaluation process developed by Tyler (1949), which focused on determining the congruence between program objectives and learner outcomes, was predominant until the 1960s. This process is presently seen as one of many possible approaches, with approximately forty formal evaluation models represented in the published literature (Nevo, 1983). This literature on education evaluation is much too comprehensive to summarize briefly. Useful overviews of the entire evaluation process and the different approaches to evaluation may be found in Anderson and Ball (1978); Cordray, Bloom, and Light (1987); and Worthen and Sanders (1973). Thoughtful advice is also available on utilization-focused evaluation (Patton, 1978) and naturalistic approaches to evaluation (Guba and Lincoln, 1981). Some of the most useful approaches to evaluation from the field of adult and continuing education include Grotelueschen (1980), Knox (1979), Deshler (1984), and Sork, Kalef, and Worsfold (1987). In the specific field of continuing professional education the writings of Knox (1985a), Levine, Moore, and Pennington (1984), LeBreton and others (1979), and Grotelueschen (1986) are helpful.

These references offer many excellent descriptions of the goals, methods, and processes of program evaluation, which can be applied with equal validity to continuing professional education as to any other educational endeavor.

A Framework of Evaluation Questions

The framework offered here has several antecedents in the evaluation literature. Suchman (1967) wrote from the perspective of an evaluation specialist, while Kirkpatrick (1975), Bennett (1975), and Houle (1980) are continuing educators who deal respectively with the fields of training, cooperative extension, and continuing professional education. The framework used in this chapter (which has appeared in a different version elsewhere [Cervero, 1984a]), suggests seven categories of evaluation questions organized around the following criteria: program design and implementation; learner participation; learner satisfaction; learner knowledge, skills, and attitudes; application of learning after the program; the impact of application of learning; and program characteristics associated with outcomes.

Evaluative information collected in one category is not inherently better or more useful than information collected in another category. The seven categories should be viewed as a hierarchy only in the sense that the evaluative information gathered at one level should not be used to infer success or failure at other levels. For example, if learners express satisfaction with a program, their satisfaction does not imply changes in knowledge, skills, or attitudes.

The author worked with the nursing education staff of a 500-bed medical center hospital in Chicago to evaluate a continuing education program (Cervero and Rottet, 1984). The program, which included thirty-three hours of classroom instruction over six weeks, was designed to prepare forty-seven recently hired registered nurses for practice at the hospital. Clinical instruction during the nurses' practice was used extensively to complement the classroom work. This evaluation design was replicated when the same program was offered the following year (Cervero, Rottet, and Dimmock, 1986). Data were collected to answer evaluation questions from four of the seven evaluation categories. Examples of evaluation questions and strategies are drawn from these data.

Program Design and Implementation. This category of questions assesses what was planned, what was actually implemented, and the congruence between these two dimensions. Commonly asked questions revolve around such factors as the activities of learners and instructors and the adequacy of the physical environment for facilitating learning. In the nursing education study, information was not systematically collected for these questions; however, answers to the following questions were informally sought: Did the instructors cover all of the material? Was the program design working in terms of a correlation between the classroom instruction and the clinical instruction on the hospital units? How much time was allocated to participant discussion? Was the design of the classroom conducive to effective learning?

The importance of these types of evaluation questions is illustrated by Levine, Moore, and Pennington (1984, pp. 209–215), who identify nineteen major issues that guide the evaluation of continuing health education programs (most of which are relevant to all professions). Nine of these questions relate to program design and implementation, including: Does the planned activity clearly relate to identified community health needs? Are the selection, orientation, and motivation of faculty effective? Did the intended instructional activities operate as planned?

Such evaluative questions as these are often asked about programs, although more often than not the resulting information is not collected systematically. The questions are often answered anecdotally, with information provided by the instructor or collected in hallway conversations with participants. Such information becomes more useful when it is collected systematically. Three groups — participants, instructors, and program planners — possess a unique perspective, and several systematic techniques, including questionnaires, interviews, and observational rating scales, can be used to collect relevant information. For example, if the program developer wants to know whether all the planned topics are covered, how much time is spent on each, and what methods are used, both participants and instructors can complete a questionnaire that deals with these questions at the end of each day of instruction. During the first program offering, the director of nursing education can be a participant-observer and use a rating scale to collect this information. Interviewing several participants at the close of the program is another strategy that can be employed. Generally, these strategies require a small amount of effort but tend to produce quite useful evaluative data.

The implementation process almost always contains unknowns that change the program design. Since the actual program may be quite different from its design on paper, it is important to know how far the program has deviated from the design and in what ways. The instructor or the program planner can judge whether any adjustments need to be made for the next program offering.

Learner Participation. Most observers agree that the most common type of evaluation questions concerns learner participation (Houle, 1980, p. 238; Clegg, 1987). This should not be surprising, for two reasons: (1) most programs can only be conducted if there are enough participants, and (2) these questions are relatively easy to answer. This second category of evaluation questions has both quantitative and qualitative dimensions. The quantitative dimension contains probably the most common evaluative question asked of any formal program: How many participants attended the program? This is certainly one way to judge the work of a program. If many professionals choose to spend their time in this program, it must have promised something of value to them. Collecting data to answer this question is simple: A record of how many participants attended the activity is usually available through the formal registration process or from a sign-up sheet. Although this kind of evaluation question has been roundly criticized (for example, Houle, 1980, pp. 242–243), the answer is nonetheless important for many continuing professional educators. The question is appropriate as long as these data are not used to infer answers to questions in the other categories, such as whether the learners were satisfied with the program or whether they learned something.

Another question that can be asked in the quantitative dimension of this category is (Levine, Moore, and Pennington, 1984): Did the practitioners who attended the program have the background and experience that were anticipated when the program was planned? This particular question was important in the nursing education evaluation because the program was planned for nurses who were fresh out of school. It might have been less relevant for those who had significant amounts of experience. Comparing the characteristics of actual versus expected participants is fairly easy. For example, if all of the participants were expected to be new graduates and only half who actually attended were, a clear planning problem has been revealed. Another question that can often provide useful information is: What proportion of the participants stayed for the entire program? This can be particularly appropriate for programs that last longer than one day.

Qualitative types of questions can also be asked about learner participation. In order to judge learners' reactions to a program, continuing educators often try to assess the degree to which the participants were involved or engaged in the flow of the program. This information is usually collected in an anecdotal fashion by unobtrusively observing the proceedings of the educational activity. However, the information would be more useful if it were collected systematically by, for example, asking the instructor to complete a brief questionnaire or to write a narrative statement at the end of the program. A participant-observer, such as the program planner, could also provide this information.

Although questions relating to learner participation tend to be overemphasized in judgments of a program's worth, they are important for several reasons. First, a minimum level of participation is often required to justify offering a continuing education program. Second, the number of participants in a program can change its effectiveness — too few or too many participants can be detrimental to achieving its objectives. Third, the extent to which participants are actively engaged in the program can also influence its effectiveness. If answers to these types of questions are needed by decision makers, then this may be sufficient reason to ask them.

Learner Satisfaction. The second most common way to judge the worth of a continuing professional education program is to collect evidence about learners' satisfaction according to various elements, such as content, educational process, instructor, physical facilities, and cost. The most commonly offered rationale for this type of evaluation question is that "professionals are particularly well-equipped by their sophistication to make decisions about the quality of their instruction" (Houle, 1980, p. 244). Grotelueschen (1986) amplifies this argument by saying that professionals are "qualified to judge the value of educational endeavors designed to enhance their own development" (p. 2) due to their many years of training and native intelligence.

Some typical evaluation questions in this category are: In general, do you think the topics were adequately covered? Did the sequencing of topics promote your learning effectively? To what extent was the instructor organized? and Was the physical environment conducive to learning? Although information required to answer these questions is sometimes collected anecdotally, using a systematic method can increase confidence in its validity and reliability. One method often used for longer programs involves selecting a representative sample of participants from the total group. This is often effective if participants select their own representatives — usually between three and five — at the beginning of the program. This group can provide continuous evaluation throughout the program regarding issues of interest to the instructor and participants. The members of this group can be asked to keep their eyes and ears open for reactions from other learners, to poll their fellow learners systematically, to react to evaluative questions on the basis of their own perceptions, or to engage in any combination of these activities.

Perhaps the most common method is the end-of-program questionnaire, in which participants respond to a series of open-ended or fixed-response questions. This method was used for the nursing education evaluation in obtaining answers to several evaluation questions, such as the relevance of the program to the participants' practice, the effectiveness of the faculty, and the match between the program's educational strategies and participants' learning style (Cervero and Rottet, 1984). The primary benefits of this method are that it is relatively inexpensive, information can be collected quickly and uniformly, and responses can be given anonymously. Anonymity is important because it reduces the likelihood of bias toward socially desirable responses. A weakness of this method is that the validity of evaluative information depends largely on the quality of the questionnaire's construction. Questions that are interpreted by respondents in different ways produce useless data. Kidder (1981) presents a detailed guide to questionnaire construction that can help increase the validity and reliability of this data collection procedure.

One of the most conceptually sound and most adequately tested approaches to evaluating learner satisfaction has been developed by Grotelueschen (1986). This approach is organized around what Grotelueschen defines as the four essential elements of any continuing professional education program: presenters, content, participants, and setting. He has developed a number of different formats that can be selected, depending on the length of the program, the estimated number of participants, and the number of session presenters. Formats are specifically designed for the two- to three-day short course, the half-day session, and the fifty- to sixty-minute mini-sessions at conferences.

It is wise to interpret learner satisfaction data cautiously, especially when no other data are collected. Studies have shown that learner satisfaction can be unrelated or even negatively related to learning (Houle, 1980, p. 245; Naftulin, Ware, and Donnelly, 1973). Learner satisfaction is not a surrogate for how much learning occurred. On the positive side, questions about learner satisfaction are important because professionals have different reasons for participating (Grotelueschen, 1985) and different teaching format preferences. Accordingly, success can have multiple definitions within a single program, and learner satisfaction data can reveal the variety of definitions that are used to judge the success of a program (Warmuth, 1987).

Learner Knowledge, Skills, and Attitudes. This category of evaluative questions focuses on changes in learners' cognitive, affective, or psychomotor competence. Questions of this type were popularized by Tyler (1949) and have been widely used since then at all levels of education. In evaluating the nursing education program, the questions in this category included: Do the participants know the hospital's legal guidelines related to the performance of nursing functions? Can they appropriately document nursing care in the patient's records? and What are their attitudes toward nursing practice and continuing education?

The designs for this type of evaluation have been highly developed for conventional forms of schooling and have been succinctly summarized by Houle (1980, p. 247). Program objectives are stated in terms of what the learner is expected to know or be able to do. The objectives are often stated in behavioral terms so that their accomplishment can either be evaluated directly or give rise to evaluative criteria (Mager, 1975). A system of measurement is devised that permits such evaluation. This system often includes a pretest to determine the learners' knowledge or ability at the beginning of the program. The same measurement is made at the end of the program, and the pre- and posttest data are compared to determine whether change has occurred. Judgments are then made about the effectiveness of the program.

The method of measurement used most often within this category is the paper-and-pencil test. Gronlund (1982) provides a useful set of procedures for constructing achievement tests in the cognitive domain, and similar guidelines are available for other individual professions, such as engineering (Cole and others, 1984). Kidder (1981) presents a variety of methods for assessing attitudes, such as questionnaires, interviews, projective tests, play techniques, psychodrama, and sociodrama. Each of these methods has its strengths and weaknesses, which must be considered when choosing among them. Green and Walsh (1979) describe several techniques for assessing changes in skills, such as role playing in a simulated environment and the use of videotapes and motion pictures. These evaluation techniques provide information only about what participants do in settings divorced from real life.

Some continuing educators have resisted using tests as a way of evaluating their programs. This attitude may have arisen because of the extensive use of testing procedures in formal schooling settings, from which many continuing educators wish to disassociate themselves. Be that as it may, there is nothing inherently unsound in the use of testing to evaluate continuing professional education programs. Testing can be accomplished well or poorly, it can be a natural part of the learning process or a contrived barrier to learning, and it can precipitate negative memories of preservice education or meet the universal need for feedback. The important issue is not testing per se, but rather the methods used to collect the information, the relationship between the testing process and the educational process, and the intended and actual uses of the information.

Application of Learning After the Program. Educational programs are temporary, artificial environments that require learners to remove themselves from their natural environments to acquire new capabilities. This category of evaluative questions addresses the degree to which the knowledge, skills, and attitudes learned during the program are applied in the learners' natural environment. This type of evaluation question has been considered so important that comprehensive reviews of the published literature have been conducted in several professions, including medicine (Brooks and Brooks-Bertram, 1977; Lloyd and Abrahamson, 1979; Hayes and others, 1984; Raymond, 1986), nursing (Gosnell, 1984), and engineering (Kaufman, 1977). The primary question asked in the nursing education evaluations was the extent to which the nurses applied their learning, which was measured immediately after the program and again six months later.

The evaluative information in this category is almost always collected after the program. Unlike testing, in which the educator controls the conditions under which data are collected, assessments of application are much more difficult to control. One must wait to collect the evaluative information until program participants have produced enough data in their natural setting. In evaluating the nursing education program, data collection could not begin until the nurses had worked with a sufficient number of patients. The difficulties inherent in collecting data on professionals' performance have led several observers to argue that this type of evaluation question can be answered most easily for educational programs sponsored by those who control the workplace (Houle, 1980, p. 249; Cervero, Rottet, and Dimmock, 1986).

Three methods of data collection are used most often to answer this category of evaluation question: self-reports, observation, and archival analysis. Asking participants to describe the extent to which they have applied their learning from the program is the least costly, but also produces the least valid results. Although some researchers have found self-reporting to be highly correlated with actual performance (Abrahamson, 1984), self-report data need to be interpreted with attention to their limitations (Kidder, 1981). In contrast, observational methods can cost much more to implement, but are potentially more valid in answering questions about learning applications. Observations can be effectively made by the learners' supervisors, co-workers, or evaluators. In the nursing education example, a trained evaluator assessed the nurses' performance and also interviewed the nurses' supervisors to collect evaluative information. The third method, archival analysis, uses written records. These same trained evaluators audited the charts of the patients on whom the learners had practiced.

Several problems make this category of evaluation questions relatively difficult to answer. First, the educational intervention must be powerful enough to produce a change in professional performance (Knox, 1985a; Sjogren, 1979). Program planners often have unrealistically high expectations in terms of what is achievable, especially for short-term programs. Unless a clear case can be made for probable impact, it is a waste of valuable resources to ask evaluation questions related to the application of learning. Another commonly encountered difficulty is that program outcomes often cannot be objectified in behavioral terms. Many factors can interfere with the transfer of learning, especially with regard to the characteristics of the work setting. These must be taken into account in any attempt to answer this category of evaluation questions.

Impact of Application of Learning. Evaluative questions in this category focus on what Grotelueschen (1980) calls second-order effects of the educational program. First-order effects are the accomplishments of those who participated in the program — for example, learners and instructors. Second-order effects are once removed from the participants. The extent to which a program for health care professionals contributes to the improved health of the public is a second-order effect. For many continuing professional educators this is the Holy Grail of evaluation questions. This type of evaluative question was not asked in the nursing education evaluation, so no direct evidence was produced regarding whether the changes in nursing performance actually made a difference in patient outcomes. To assess this type of outcome, the evaluation could have been constructed to ask whether the learners' patients were released from the hospital sooner or felt better about the care they received.

The three data collection methods described in the previous section can also be used for this category of questions. For example, the learners could have been asked in a questionnaire or an interview whether their changes in performance made a difference in patient care. More direct evidence of impact could have been obtained by comparing patient outcomes through observation and chart audits (archival analysis) for nurses who did and did not participate in the program. If there were significant differences, it could be inferred (if all other factors had been controlled) that changes in nursing performance had contributed to an improvement in patient outcomes.

This category of evaluative questions is potentially the most important because it often deals with the long-term goals of a continuing education program. Yet, answers to such questions can be the most difficult to obtain. This is less true when the program is held at a site where the participants are employed, because institutional records of performance are more readily available there. When participants come from many different work sites, evaluating the impact of the application of learning is nearly impossible except by self-report.

Apart from the availability of performance and outcome data, the most difficult problem in conducting evaluations for this and the preceding category is a conceptual one. Knox (1979, p. 118) describes the problem succinctly:

> General program characteristics can be identified that are likely to contribute to impact. One is that the program deals directly with specific and achievable changes in performance that are important to the adult learner, are amenable to educational influence, and that can be readily documented. The second is that the type and amount of educational intervention is likely to bring about the desired change. . . . Even when these two conditions are met (achievable change, reasonable intervention), it is difficult to conduct an impact study likely to prove the extent and types of benefits attributable to the program and not to other influences.

When asking evaluation questions about a program's impact on professional performance or the second-order outcomes of performance, these conditions must be considered.

Program Characteristics Associated with Outcomes. The previous six categories of evaluative questions can be grouped into two more general categories: implementation questions that address issues of program design and implementation, learner participation, and learner satisfaction; and outcome questions that address changes in knowledge, skills, and attitudes, application of learning, and impact of application of learning. Implementation questions are useful for determining what happened before and during the program. Outcome questions are useful for determining what occurred as a result of the program. If evaluation results are to provide information that can be used for program improvement, data from implementation questions should be linked with outcome data. That is, program characteristics should be associated with program outcomes. Patton describes this linkage: "Where outcomes are evaluated without knowledge of implementation, the results seldom provide direction for action because the decision-maker lacks information about what produced the observed outcomes (or lack of outcomes). This is the 'black box' approach to evaluation: Clients are tested before entering the program and after completing the program, while what happens in between is a black box" (1978, p. 155).

A conceptual framework has been developed with which to answer evaluative questions in this category, particularly for programs that seek to change professional performance or client outcomes (Cervero, 1985). The framework proposes that four sets of variables affect the extent of performance change resulting from a continuing professional education program. These are: (1) the characteristics of the continuing education program itself, (2) the individual professional, (3) the nature of the proposed change, and (4) the social system in which the professional works. This framework was used to evaluate the nursing education program (Cervero and Rottet, 1984; Cervero, Rottet, and Dimmock, 1986) and helped to explain the variations in the nurses' application of learning after the program. It has been used in evaluating continuing education programs for nurses (Abrussese, 1987; Ruder, 1987; Rao, 1988), engineers (Brue, 1986), and public administrators (Hubbard, 1988).

It may be argued that so many relationships exist between program implementation and outcomes that it is impossible to make a truly definitive conclusion about what caused program outcomes. While this may be true in a strictly scientific sense, the alternative of not collecting any data will not improve program development efforts at all. While this type of evaluation is not commonly done, it should be used when the situation permits it. This assertion is based on the assumption that some information is better than none, as long as the limitations of the data are recognized.

Deciding on Evaluative Questions

Seven types of evaluative questions have been described in this chapter. It is not likely that a continuing professional educator will ask evaluative questions from all seven categories for a single program. Generally, the educator puzzles over which evaluative question can or should be asked. Five criteria can help educators make sound decisions regarding which questions to ask. First, what is the purpose of the educational program? Second, who needs what information for what purposes? Third, what are the practical and ethical constraints related to the evaluation effort? Fourth, what resources are available to conduct the evaluation? Fifth, what values and preferences of the educator impinge on the evaluation?

Educational programs have many purposes, which evaluation questions should address. For example, some programs are intended to increase participants' knowledge of a topic area, while others are intended to have second-order effects. If planners intend a program to change professional performance, the evaluation questions should focus on the application of learning after the program. In other cases a program's purpose might be to change learners' attitudes, so the evaluation should focus on that, rather than on the impact of attitude change on the learners' co-workers. Thus, one type of evaluation question is better than another only to the extent that it corresponds to the program's purposes.

Any evaluation should be planned so that its results are used (Patton, 1978). To increase the likelihood that evaluation results will be used educators should determine who is likely to use the information and what kinds of information those persons need. The users of the results should be involved as much as possible in the evaluation design, implementation, and analysis because their involvement in the process increases the likelihood that the findings will be used. There are five important groups of users of evaluative information: program participants, instructors, program planners, those who finance the participants' attendance (for example, employers), and administrators of the sponsoring institution. Each group may have different information needs. For example, the instructor may wish to know whether the participants have offered suggestions on how to improve her teaching. The program planner may be concerned primarily with whether the program was implemented as planned. Those who financed the participants' attendance may want to know whether their learning was applied at the workplace. The evaluation may need to address all of these questions. However, if none of these people would use the evaluation results, there is probably no need to evaluate the program.

Both practical and ethical constraints related to the evaluation process affect the kinds of questions that can be asked. For instance, program participants may not want their performance on the job to be observed, or it may not be feasible to do so for other reasons. Anderson and Ball (1978) discuss a number of ethical considerations that affect the types of evaluations that are conducted. These issues include the confidentiality of data and the proper relationships between the program planner, funding agent, and evaluator.

Grotelueschen (1980) discusses several categories of resources that should be considered in planning an evaluation. The availability of these resources should be determined before the questions are finally formulated. These resources include money to pay for supplies and services, staff time for such things as interviews and data analysis, and the expertise needed to conduct the evaluation. The evaluation often consumes resources that could be used for other purposes, so it is important to ascertain what resources are available and how willing people are to use them for evaluation.

Finally, the evaluator's own preferences and values have an effect on the types of evaluation questions asked (Anderson and Ball, 1978). For example, if the instructor is also the evaluator, he will have a particular set of biases as well as helpful insights about the program design and implementation. Also, some educators may feel that one type of analytical technique, such as statistical analysis, is more appropriate than others. The evaluation questions may need to be posed in such a way that the results can be subjected to statistical analysis. It is impossible to expunge these values and preferences; rather, one should make them explicit so that everyone involved in the evaluation process is aware of their influence.

Evaluation processes must be part of the larger cycle of program development, just as program development is a form of professional practice. Evaluation problems, like program planning problems, are encountered in situations that are characterized by uniqueness, uncertainty, and value conflicts. By using the examples, images, and understandings from their repertoires, continuing educators can determine the evaluation problems to be solved as well as how to solve them.

▼

CHAPTER 9

Being Effective
in Continuing
Professional
Education

THROUGHOUT THIS BOOK an attempt has been made to identify the elements of effective practice in continuing professional education. These elements include the ethical dimensions of practice (Chapter Two), concepts of professionals both as learners and participants (Chapters Three and Four), the institutional context of practice (Chapters Five and Six), and approaches to program development and evaluation (Chapters Seven and Eight). Although these elements may be separated for analytical purposes, they do not exist in isolation in the real world of practice. Continuing educators see professionals as learners and as participants as they develop and evaluate programs, which they do within an institutional context and a particular ethical framework. Because these elements operate simultaneously in most practice situations, they must be synthesized into a coherent whole to understand and to improve practice.

In this final chapter these various elements are synthesized into a unified picture of effective practice in continuing professional education. The purpose is to offer a comprehensive statement of what constitutes effective practice, thereby providing the criteria to evaluate and improve current efforts in continuing professional education. These criteria may be used to evaluate individual or collective activities of many continuing educators working with any of the professional groups identified in Chapter One.

Continuing Educators as Professionals

The identification and analysis of the elements of effective practice flow from the assumption that continuing educators are engaged in a form of professional practice. This assumption was acknowledged at the end of Chapter Seven when program development was described as a form of professional work. This premise is now made explicit in order to explore its implications. The foundations of this exploration are the discussions of professional practice and knowledge in Chapters Two and Three. Thus, an understanding of effective practice for continuing professional educators should be consistent with the view of effectiveness in all forms of professional practice.

As discussed in Chapter Two, the functionalist, conflict, and critical viewpoints provide three fundamentally different understandings of professional practice. It was argued that the critical viewpoint offers the most accurate understanding of professional practice and should form the foundation of understanding continuing professional educators' practice. In choosing the critical viewpoint the functionalist and conflict viewpoints were rejected because they offer incomplete descriptions of practice.

Functionalist prescriptions for effective practice offer suggestions for good practice in such areas as assessing needs, developing objectives, assessing learning outcomes, and administrating institutional units. These prescriptions are generally in the form of guidelines or principles that are to be applied to situations faced by continuing educators. Take, for example, that shibboleth of good practice, assessing the needs of learners. The principle is often stated something like this: Sponsors of continuing education programs should utilize systematic processes to define and analyze the issues or problems of individuals, groups, and organizations for the purpose of determining learning needs. While this may seem like a worthwhile goal for practice, it offers little in the way of guidance to practitioners because it ignores the crucial element of institutional context.

To be sure, there is no shortage of statements of good practice that provide what must seem a rather obvious list of things continuing educators ought to be able to do. However, the existence of such lists assumes that there are standard contexts and problems to which these principles can be applied. Herein lies the fatal flaw, for, as discussed in Chapter Five, continuing educators work in a variety of different situations that make radically different demands on their skills, knowledge, and judgment. One of the fundamental problems in conceiving of effective practice as the application of principles to situations is that each principle means different things and emerges as different practices in varying contexts. A major reason, then, that continuing educators reject textbook prescriptions for exemplary practice is that the principles are either vacuous (because they have to apply to all continuing educators, regardless of their circumstances) or limited (because they discount the details of the context), or both (Sockett, 1987).

To illustrate these points, take the example (in Chapter Two) in which the continuing educator is planning a program for engineers on new techniques for designing nuclear power plants. The question to answer is: What would effective practice look like in terms of assessing the needs for this program? An important consideration in answering this question is the type of institution in which the continuing educator works. The context of a university continuing education unit provides a different set of constraints and opportunities for the educator than the power plant does for the training director (Table 2 reviews these). For example, the training director has direct access to the learners themselves, as well as records of their performance. Another consideration is the level of resources that the educator has available to conduct the needs assessment. Suppose the university continuing educator responds to a request from the training director for a program on the newest techniques in designing power plants. The educator knows that the training director did not conduct a systematic needs assessment and that no university resources are available to conduct one. Should his practice be judged as ineffective in this situation? What criteria would be used to do so?

Even this brief example should be sufficient to point out the shortcomings of the functionalist understanding of continuing education practice. Instead, as argued at the end of Chapter Two, continuing professional educators must operate within the critical viewpoint in order to provide a comprehensive understanding of continuing education practice and the means to improve it. The critical viewpoint asserts that practice cannot be understood as the application of standardized principles to well-formed problems because most situations faced by continuing educators are characterized by uniqueness, uncertainty, or value conflict. Like other professionals, continuing educators must make choices about the nature of the problem to be solved as well as how to solve it. Because continuing educators are continually making choices, as opposed to simply applying principles, the critical viewpoint stresses the need to be aware of the range of choices open to educators and the ways in which these can be made. The critical viewpoint provides a framework within which to describe effective practice in continuing professional education. It offers a rich account of practice and one that can help continuing educators to improve their work.

Understanding Effective Practice

Continuing educators' practice must be rooted in a coherent account of its ethical, contextual, and epistemological bases. All of these bases of practice are interconnected and are implicit in all forms of practice in which continuing educators engage. The next sections discuss each of the bases in more detail.

Ethical Basis of Practice. Because they seek to change individuals through their programs, continuing professional educators, like all educators, are engaged in a normative enterprise. Any attempt to change professionals is based on ideals of what they ought to be, to know, to do, or to feel. These ideals are rooted in continuing educators' beliefs about the goodness or rightness of the new course of action. Herein lies the ethical nature of practice, for educators continually make choices, often implicitly, about the ideals toward which their activities are directed. Therefore, practice can be judged as effective only with respect to a particular ethical framework, and it can be judged as ineffective if it is inconsistent with the tenets of the framework by which it is being evaluated.

Many continuing professional educators act as if there is consensus about the proper ends of professional practice. As a result, there is rarely any discussion of the ethical dimensions of their practice. Continuing educators are often blinded to the ethical implications of their work by the homogeneous value orientations of the environments in which they work. They are often unaware that they make ethical choices in their practice because everyone who may be involved in a particular situation agrees with those choices. Stripped of this ethical understanding, continuing educators are limited to using a paratechnical language to describe their practice, using words such as needs assessment, performance objectives, collaboration, and teaching style. This provides at least a partial explanation for the current dominance of the functionalist understanding of professional practice.

In all professions there are differing, if not conflicting, ethical frameworks that guide the work of practitioners. Examples were provided in Chapter Two. In the same way, continuing educators' practice is embedded in a variety of ethical frameworks. Every educative activity for which continuing educators have responsibility is a statement about the need for a particular form of technical knowledge, as well as a statement about the proper ends of professional practice. The ethical questions that are central to educational practice are: Why should professionals have this knowledge? To what ends will this knowledge be put? and What model of the learner should guide educational decisions? The most important decisions continuing educators must make in order to answer these questions are: Who should decide on the content of the activity? and On the basis of what criteria?

These ethical choices are not some abstract ideal, but are embedded in the very fabric of practice. Let us return to the continuing engineering education example in which the training director has asked the university continuing educator for a program on the newest techniques in designing nuclear power plants. By agreeing to deliver this program, the educator has made a series of ethical choices. For example, he believes that building power plants is a good thing and that the engineers need new knowledge to build them. He may not acknowledge having made these choices; instead, he might say he is basing his decision to offer the program on the need to generate income for the university continuing education unit. However, he cannot deny that the content of the program is consistent with a particular ideal about what society needs. His practice would be seen as effective if one agreed with this ideal and if the engineers attended the program and learned the new engineering techniques. However, his practice would be seen as ineffective if one did not agree with this ideal; for example, if participation in the program facilitated the goal of building nuclear power plants, and if one were opposed to nuclear power, then this practice would be seen as ineffective.

Our understanding of continuing education practice is impoverished by not discussing its ethical dimensions. Ethical understanding is central to the practice of all professionals and is an important criterion by which decisions are made in many situations. If continuing educators are to adequately understand and improve their practice, its ethical dimensions must be made explicit in the context of their own practical knowledge, as well as in the ongoing discussions of good practice in the continuing education literature.

Contextual Basis of Practice. Continuing education practice is not conducted in a laboratory where all conditions are controlled except for the educator's actions. If this were true it would be reasonable to construct a description of ideal practices, the completion of which would produce specified results. As we know, however, practice is always conducted in a context composed of varying personalities, shifting expectations, conflicting goals, and limited resources. Because continuing educators' practice is rooted in particular sets of circumstances, it would be inappropriate to judge their efforts against some fixed ideal of good practice. Rather, to know whether practice is effective it must be judged by what is best in a given set of circumstances. Excellent practice cannot be characterized by a discrete set of knowledge of skills, but rather by an understanding of why educators do what they do when they do it. At the root of practice is not measurable techniques but judgment, which is itself a form of knowledge (Sockett, 1987).

The primary context for continuing educators is provided by the institutional setting in which they practice. Continuing educators are not independent agents developing educative activities in ways they alone believe to be the most appropriate. Rather, their concepts of a target audience, how best to serve it, and what resources are available are conditioned by their particular institutional contexts. Their work is conducted within a discretionary framework set up by the goals and resources of the agency in which they work. As described in Chapter Five, there are four principal types of institutional contexts in which continuing professional education is provided. The continuing education unit in which practitioners work will have different functions depending on the type of institution in which it is located. Thus, its effectiveness will be judged in different ways. For example, many employing agencies use continuing education to improve professionals' performance, while others use it to generate income. Some of these functions may not seem ideal and may even contradict an educator's own vision of what constitutes effective practice. Yet, within an institutional context, these different functions help to define the circumstances within which educators practice.

The contextual relativity of practice does not mean that all practice is equally good. It does mean that practice can only be judged against what is best under the circumstances in which it occurs. Returning to the continuing engineering education example, let us ask whether the university-based continuing educator should have assessed the learning needs of the target audience. Let us assume that the training director asks for a program on the newest techniques of nuclear power plant design. To decide whether and what kind of needs assessment is required in this situation, more information is required. That alone illustrates the contextually relevant nature of the decision. It is easy to conceive of a set of circumstances in which the educator should have done a systematic needs assessment but did not. Perhaps a course is taught on design techniques that cannot be implemented in the engineers' work setting. This continuing educator clearly can be judged as having engaged in ineffective practice.

It is possible to develop guidelines that can serve as orienting principles for effective practice. However, these guidelines must be *models of* practice in the sense that   are taken from studies of actual practice. The guidelines will prove useless if they are *models for* continuing practice, in the sense of prescriptions of how educators ought to conduct themselves regardless of the specific context. If guidelines are to be used to judge practice, the criteria must be developed out of the actual situation being evaluated. Context is not an adjunct to understanding effective practice; rather, it is woven into the very fabric of practice.

Epistemological Basis of Practice. To fully explain effective practice, continuing educators must be able to describe how they do what they do. This description provides an understanding of the epistemological basis of their practice. The question that is of central concern here is: "What kind of knowledge or knowing characterizes effective practice? Another way to say this is: What does one need to know to be an effective practitioner? Schön (1983, 1987) has answered these questions by offering an epistemology of professional artistry.

An epistemology (such as technical rationality) that can only offer an account of the declarative knowledge possessed by continuing educators is inadequate as a tool for understanding the complexity of practice. The program planning frameworks described in Chapter Seven are examples of declarative knowledge about continuing professional education. This type of epistemology does not adequately describe the forms of knowledge that distinguish the excellent educator from the merely adequate, or in Benner's (1984) terms, the expert from the novice. For example, many expert continuing educators cannot describe any one of the planning frameworks from Chapter Seven, whereas many novices can describe them in great detail. A more appropriate epistemology is needed to connect continuing educators' plans, techniques, ideals, and knowledge to the real judgments made in the unique, uncertain, and changing contexts of practice.

Schön responds to this need by suggesting that two forms of knowing are central to effective practice: knowing-in-action and reflection-in-action. In contrast to the epistemology that views practice as the application of knowledge, Schön assumes that continuing educators' knowing is in their actions. Many of their spontaneous actions do not stem from a rule or plan they were conscious of before their action. That is, continuing educators constantly make judgments for which they cannot state a rule or theory. In many cases this knowing-in-action does not solve a particular problem because the situations faced by continuing educators are unique, uncertain, or marked by conflicting values. Therefore, they need to construct the situation to make it solvable. The ability to do this, to reflect-in-action, is the core of effective practice.

Returning to our example, how did the university-based continuing educator decide whether or not to conduct a needs assessment for the continuing engineering education program? If Schön's analysis is correct, the continuing educator would make the best judgment under the circumstances if he were highly skilled at reflecting-in-action. What would this process look like? The assumption is that this is an indeterminate situation because it is not immediately obvious that a needs assessment should be conducted. The continuing educator's goal is to change this situation into a determinate one, one in which he is relatively certain about the correct course of action. Based on past experience, the educator has built up a repertoire of examples and understandings of situations like this. This repertoire of practical knowledge is used to make sense of the current situation, to see it as some prior situation in which his actions were successful. Once the current situation is framed in such a way as to make it solvable, the educator would probably conduct an on-the-spot experiment to test its appropriateness. This might be done during conversations with others, such as the training director or the head of the continuing education unit, to determine their satisfaction with the potential course of action.

If effective practice is not to be utterly context-dependent, its epistemology must account for a kind of knowing that can be used in most or all situations. Reflection-in-action is such an epistemology. Its use is a key to understanding effective practice in continuing professional education. This epistemology describes how continuing educators make decisions in areas such as developing and evaluating educative activities, fostering participation in such activities, and forming interorganizational relationships. For instance, the entire program development process may be viewed as a form of reflection-in-action in which educators are continually framing ambiguous situations so as to make them solvable. Specific criteria for framing and making evaluation decisions (such as the purpose of the educational program) were suggested at the end of Chapter Eight. Also, criteria for framing and making decisions about interorganizational relationships (such as motivators and costs) were offered at the end of Chapter Six. And Chapter Four offered a set of considerations, such as professionals' reasons for participation in continuing education, that can inform judgments about how to foster participation in specific situations.

The interrelationship of the ethical, contextual, and epistemological bases of effective practice can be articulated as follows: *Effective practice in continuing professional education means making the best judgment in a specific context and for a specified ethical framework.* These judgments, which are made as a result of knowing-in-action and reflection-in-action, are evaluated as best against what is possible in the specific circumstances in which they occur and what is desirable within a particular ethical framework.

Improving Practice

To improve practice, the abilities of continuing educators to make their "best judgements" must be facilitated. How can the ability to judge be facilitated by those who train continuing professional educators and by those educators themselves? To improve suggests a process of learning and thus, as discussed in Chapter Three, this facilitation must be based on a model of continuing educators as learners. As with other professionals, it is essential to specify how they know and how they acquire this knowledge.

Continuing educators' knowing-in-action is acquired from their reflection-in-action undertaken in the indeterminate zones of practice and from the theory and research developed in continuing education and other fields. Reflection-in-action generates new knowledge by contributing new examples, understandings, and actions to educators' already existing repertoires. The acquisition of reflection-in-action appears to be less straightforward than the acquisition of knowing-in-action. Continuing educators reflect-in-action as a matter of course in their everyday life and use these same processes in their practice. However, to improve this ability continuing educators must reflect on their reflection-in-action by describing what they have done. As they can more consciously describe how they reflect and what that teaches them, continuing educators can more readily employ that form of knowing in new situations.

Practice can also be improved by participating in formal educational programs. In formal educational settings, such as conferences, workshops, and graduate programs in continuing education, declarative knowledge about continuing professional education is most often stressed. To increase the likelihood that this knowledge will be incorporated into continuing educators' practice, it must be presented in such a way that continuing educators will use it to reflect on their own practice situations in the presence of the instructor. This type of process can build the educators' repertoires of practical knowledge. Experientially based methods, such as case studies, simulations, and role plays, are useful for developing this kind of knowledge. Practice can also be improved in these settings by helping continuing educators increase their ability to reflect-in-action. Schön's (1987) suggestive account of how this process can be coached, but not taught, is useful. Faculty in graduate programs and workshop presenters, for example, can assume the role of coaches by explaining how they would perform in given practice situations and by reflecting with participants on the ways in which they approach similar situations.

The primary responsibility for improving practice in work settings falls to continuing educators themselves. The major strategy is for continuing educators to see themselves as researchers of their own practice. Their goal should be to understand how they frame problems and their own roles, to uncover their own practical knowledge and the processes by which they use that knowledge. Individual reflections on practice can be fostered by institutionally supported activities, such as staff meetings where practitioners discuss how their practice is affected by the constraints of their organizational settings. A tremendous amount of practical knowledge generally exists in a collection of continuing educators at the workplace, which unfortunately is often not fully tapped by others. Supervisors often have a wealth of uncovered practical knowledge among their staff that is not systematically made available to everyone. Finding ways to identify and share this knowledge would offer many ways to improve the practice of individual educators, as well as the collective work of a given continuing education unit.

Continuing professional education researchers also have a role to play in improving practice. Their theoretical formulations and empirical studies have an important role in improving practice. However, much more effort and resources need to be expended in these efforts in order to improve practice. More research and development units need to be developed, such as the one at Pennsylvania State University, where a collection of researchers focuses on a particular area of continuing professional education. This could be done by any one of the four principal providers of continuing professional education or through the collaborative efforts of several providers. Some of their work should begin to focus on continuing educators' practical knowledge and the processes these practitioners use to make the best judgments, the effect of context on these judgments, and the ethical frameworks in which these judgments are made. Researchers can do this by examining their own practice as continuing educators or by working collaboratively with practitioners. Benner (1984), Elbaz (1983), and Schön (1983) have offered useful ways to conduct this type of research.

Much of this book has focused on ways for individual continuing professional educators to understand and improve their own practice. However, this book is based on the premise that continuing educators in all the professions are working on similar educational processes and issues. Although the responsibility for improving practice must rest ultimately with individual continuing educators, the achievement of this goal can be facilitated by individuals who see themselves as part of the collective enterprise of continuing professional education.

REFERENCES

Abrahamson, S. "Evaluation of Continuing Education in the Health Professions: The State of the Art." *Evaluation and the Health Professions*, 1984, *7*, 3–23.

Abrussese, R. S. "The Cervero Model." *The Journal of Continuing Education in Nursing*, 1987, *18*, 33–34.

Ade, W. "Professionalization and Its Implications for the Field of Early Childhood Education." *Young Children*, 1982, *37*, 25–32.

Akintade, A. A. "An Investigation of the Factors Deterring Participation in Continuing Professional Education." Unpublished doctoral dissertation, Department of Education, North Texas State University, 1985.

American Institute of Certified Public Accountants. *Position Paper on Mandatory Continuing Professional Education for the Accounting Profession*. New York: American Institute of Certified Public Accountants, September 1985.

Anderson, J. R. *The Architecture of Cognition*. Cambridge, Mass.: Harvard University Press, 1983.

Anderson, R. E., and Kasl, E.S. (eds.). *The Costs and Financing of Adult Education and Training*. Lexington, Mass.: Heath, 1982.

Anderson, S. B., and Ball, S. *The Profession and Practice of Program Evaluation*. San Francisco: Jossey-Bass, 1978.

Apps, J. W. *Improving Practice in Continuing Education: Modern Approaches for Understanding the Field and Determining Priorities*. San Francisco: Jossey-Bass, 1985.

Arends, R. I. "Beginning Teachers as Learners." *Journal of Educational Research*, 1983, *76*, 235–242.

Argyris, C., and Schön, D. A. *Theory in Practice: Increasing Professional Effectiveness*. San Francisco: Jossey-Bass, 1974.

Armstrong, R. J. "Adult Development, Career Stage and Selected Demographics and the Continuing Education of United Presbyterian Pastors in a Three-State Area (Michigan, Ohio, Kentucky)." Unpublished doctoral dissertation, Department of Education, Ohio State University, 1983.

161

Arnstein, G. E. "The Federal Interest." In M. R. Stern (ed.), *Power and Conflict in Continuing Professional Education.* Belmont, Calif.: Wadsworth, 1983.

Azzaretto, J. F. "Competitive Strategy in Continuing Professional Education." In C. Baden (ed.), *Competitive Strategies for Continuing Education.* New Directions for Continuing Education, no. 35. San Francisco: Jossey-Bass, 1987.

Baldwin, R. "Adult and Career Development: What Are the Implications for Faculty." In American Association for Higher Education (ed.), *Current Issues in Higher Education: Faculty Career Development.* Washington, D.C.: American Association for Higher Education, 1979.

Barber, B. "Some Problems in the Sociology of the Professions." *Daedalus,* 1963, *92,* 669–688.

Barham, P. M., and Benseman, J. "Participation in Continuing Medical Education of General Practitioners in New Zealand." *Journal of Medical Education,* 1984, *59,* 649–654.

Baskett, H. K. "Continuing Professional Education in Social Work: An Examination of Knowledge Utilisation from a Field Perspective." Unpublished doctoral dissertation, Department of Education. University of Sussex, 1983.

Baskett, H. K., and Taylor, W. H. (eds.). *Continuing Professional Education: Moving into the 1980's.* Calgary, Alberta: The University of Calgary, 1980.

Becker, H. S. "The Nature of a Profession." In N. B. Nelson (ed.), *Education for the Professions.* Chicago: University of Chicago Press, 1962.

Beder, H. W. (ed.). *Realizing the Potential of Interorganizational Cooperation.* New Directions for Continuing Education, no. 23. San Francisco: Jossey-Bass, 1984a.

Beder, H. W. "Interorganizational Cooperation: Why and How." In H. W. Beder (ed.), *Realizing the Potential of Interorganizational Cooperation.* New Directions for Continuing Education, no. 23. San Francisco: Jossey-Bass, 1984b.

Beder, H. W. "Principles for Successful Cooperation." In H. W. Beder (ed.), *Realizing the Potential of Interorganizational Cooperation.* New Directions for Continuing Education, no. 23. San Francisco: Jossey-Bass, 1984c.

Benner, P. *From Novice to Expert: Excellence and Power in Clinical*

Nursing Practice. Menlo Park, Calif.: Addison-Wesley, 1984.

Bennett, C. "Up the Hierarchy." *Journal of Extension,* 1975, *13,* 7–12.

Bennett, N. "A Method for Continuing Education Program Development in a Semirural Setting." *Journal of Allied Health,* 1979, *8,* 34–37.

Berlin, L. S. "The University and Continuing Professional Education: A Contrary View." In M. R. Stern (ed.), *Power and Conflict in Continuing Professional Education.* Belmont, Calif.: Wadsworth, 1983.

Berliner, D. C. "In Pursuit of the Expert Pedagogue." *Educational Researcher,* 1986, *15,* 5–13.

Bevis, M. E. "Role Conception and the Continuing Learning Activities of Neophyte Collegiate Nurses." Unpublished doctoral dissertation, Department of Education, University of Chicago, 1971.

Bevis, M. E. "An Instrument to Measure the Job-Time Educational Participation of Staff Nurses." *The Journal of Continuing Education in Nursing,* 1972, *3,* 24–30.

Bloom, G. F. "The Real Estate Professional." In M. R. Stern (ed.), *Power and Conflict in Continuing Professional Education.* Belmont, Calif.: Wadsworth, 1983.

Brookfield, S. D. *Understanding and Facilitating Adult Learning: A Comprehensive Analysis of Principles and Effective Practices.* San Francisco: Jossey-Bass, 1986.

Brooks, D. A., and Brooks-Bertram, P. A. "The Evaluation of Continuing Medical Education: A Literature Review." *Health Education Monographs,* 1977, *5,* 330–362.

Brown, C. R., and Uhl, H. S. M. "Mandatory Continuing Education: Sense or Nonsense." *Journal of the American Medical Association,* 1970, *213,* 1660–1668.

Bruce, J. D., Siebert, W. M., Smullin, L. D., and Fano, R. M. *Lifelong Cooperative Education.* Cambridge, Mass.: Massachusetts Institute of Technology, 1982.

Brue, A. E. "Analysis of the Effectiveness of a Continuing Professional Education Program on Performance Outcomes of Engineers." Unpublished doctoral dissertation, Department of Leadership and Educational Policy Studies, Northern Illinois University, 1986.

Bruner, J. "Models of the Learner." *Educational Researcher,*

1985, *14*, 5–8.
Bucher, R., and Strauss, A. "Professions in Process." *American Journal of Sociology*, 1961, *66*, 325–334.
Canadian Journal of University Continuing Education, 1983, *9* (2).
Carroll, J. W. "The Professional Model of Ministry—Is It Worth Saving?" *Theological Education*, 1985, *21*, 7–48.
Catlin, D. W. "An Empirical Study of Judges' Reasons for Participation in Continuing Professional Education." *Justice System Journal*, 1982, *7*, 236–256.
Cervero, R. M. "A Factor Analytic Study of Physicians' Reasons for Participating in Continuing Education." *Journal of Medical Education*, 1981, *56*, 29–34.
Cervero, R. M. "Evaluating Workshop Implementation and Outcomes." In T. J. Sork (ed.), *Designing and Implementing Effective Workshops*. New Directions for Continuing Education, no. 22. San Francisco: Jossey-Bass, 1984a.
Cervero, R. M. "Collaboration in University Continuing Professional Education." In H. W. Beder (ed.), *Realizing the Potential of Interorganizational Cooperation*. New Directions for Continuing Education, no. 23. San Francisco: Jossey-Bass, 1984b.
Cervero, R. M. "Continuing Professional Education and Behavioral Change: A Model for Research and Evaluation." *The Journal of Continuing Education in Nursing*, 1985, *16*, 85–88.
Cervero, R. M., and Dimmock, K. H. "A Factor Analytic Test of Houle's Typology of Professionals' Modes of Learning." *Adult Education Quarterly*, 1987, *37*, 125–139.
Cervero, R. M., Miller, J. D., and Dimmock, K. H. "The Formal and Informal Learning Activities of Practicing Engineers." *Engineering Education*, 1986, *77*, 112–114.
Cervero, R. M., and Rottet, S. "Analyzing the Effectiveness of Continuing Professional Education: An Exploratory Study." *Adult Education Quarterly*, 1984, *34*, 135–146.
Cervero, R. M., Rottet, S., and Dimmock, K. H. "Analyzing the Effectiveness of Continuing Professional Education at the Workplace." *Adult Education Quarterly*, 1986, *36*, 78–85.
Cervero, R. M., and Scanlan, C. L. (eds.). *Problems and Prospects in Continuing Professional Education*. New Directions for Continuing Education, no. 27. San Francisco: Jossey-Bass, 1985.
Cervero, R. M., and Young, W. H. "The Organization and

Provision of Continuing Professional Education: A Critical Review and Synthesis." In J. C. Smart (ed.), *Higher Education: Handbook of Theory and Research.* Vol. 3. New York: Agathon Press, 1987.

Charters, A. N., and Blakely, R. J. "The Management of Continuing Learning: A Model of Continuing Education as a Problem Solving Strategy for Health Manpower." In R. J. Blakely (ed.), *Fostering the Growing Need to Learn.* Rockville, Md.: Division of Regional Medical Programs, U. S. Department of Health, Education and Welfare, 1973.

Clark, C. M., and Peterson, P. L. "Teachers' Thought Processes." In M. C. Wittrock (ed.), *Handbook of Research on Teaching.* (3rd ed.) New York: Macmillan, 1986.

Clegg, W. H. "Management Training Evaluation: An Update." *Training and Development Journal,* 1987, *41,* 65 – 71.

Cole, H. P., and others. *Measuring Learning in Continuing Education for Engineers and Scientists.* Phoenix, Ariz.: Oryx Press, 1984.

Collert, M. E. "An Overview in Planning, Implementing, and Evaluating Continuing Nursing Education." *The Journal of Continuing Education in Nursing,* 1976, *7,* 9 – 22.

Colliver, J. A., and Osborne, C. E. "Effects of Implementation and Repeal of Mandatory CME in Illinois: A Survey of Institutional Sponsors and Physicians." Chicago: Illinois State Medical Society, August 1985.

Cooper, S. S., and Hornback, M. S. *Continuing Nursing Education.* New York: McGraw-Hill, 1973.

Cordray, D. S., Bloom, H. S., and Light, R. J. (eds.). *Evaluation Practice in Review.* New Directions for Program Evaluation, no. 34. San Francisco: Jossey-Bass, 1987.

Cross, K. P. "New Frontiers for Higher Education: Business and the Professions." In American Association for Higher Education (ed.), *Partnerships with Business and the Professions.* Washington, D.C.: American Association for Higher Education, 1981.

Cruse, R. B. "The Accounting Profession." In M. R. Stern (ed.), *Power and Conflict in Continuing Professional Education.* Belmont, Calif.: Wadsworth, 1983.

Curran, J. R. "The Professions in Banking." In M. R. Stern

(ed.), *Power and Conflict in Continuing Professional Education.* Belmont, Calif.: Wadsworth, 1983.

Dalton, G. W., Thompson, P. H., and Price, R. L. "The Four Stages of Professional Careers: A New Look at Performance by Professionals." *Organizational Dynamics,* 1977, *6,* 19–42.

Darkenwald, G. G., and Merriam, S. M. *Adult Education: Foundations of Practice.* New York: Harper & Row, 1982.

Darkenwald, G. G., and Valentine, T. "Factor Structure of Deterrents to Public Participation in Adult Education." *Adult Education Quarterly,* 1985, *35,* 177–193.

Davies, H. M., and Aquino, J. T. "Collaboration in Continuing Professional Development." *Journal of Teacher Education,* 1975, *26,* 274–277.

Day, C., and Baskett, H. K. "Discrepancies Between Intentions and Practice: Reexamining Some Basic Assumptions About Adult and Continuing Professional Education." *International Journal of Lifelong Education,* 1982, *1,* 143–155.

Derbyshire, R. C. "The Medical Profession." In M. R. Stern (ed.), *Power and Conflict in Continuing Professional Education.* Belmont, Calif.: Wadsworth, 1983.

Deshler, D. (ed.). *Evaluation for Program Improvement.* New Directions for Continuing Education, no. 24. San Francisco: Jossey-Bass, 1984.

Dewey, J. *How We Think — A Restatement of the Relation of Reflective Thinking to the Educative Process.* Lexington, Mass.: Heath, 1933.

Dickinson, G., and Verner, C. "The Provision of Inservice Education for Health Manpower." In R. J. Blakely (ed.), *Fostering the Growing Need to Learn.* Rockville, Md.: Division of Regional Medical Services, U. S. Department of Health, Education and Welfare, 1983.

Dreyfus, H. L., and Dreyfus, S. E. *Mind Over Machine.* Oxford, England: Basil Blackwell, 1986.

Ehrenreich, B., and Ehrenreich, J. "The Professional-Managerial Class." *Radical America,* 1977, *11,* 7–31.

Ehrmeyer, S. S. "Continuing Education: A Practical Programming Model for New Planners." *Journal of Allied Health,* 1980, *9,* 276-282.

Eisner, E. (ed.). *Learning and Teaching the Ways of Knowing.*

Chicago: University of Chicago Press, 1985.

Elbaz, F. "The Teacher's 'Practical Knowledge': Report of a Case Study." *Curriculum Inquiry*, 1981, *11*, 43–71.

Elbaz, F. *Teacher Thinking: A Study of Practical Knowledge.* New York: Nichols, 1983.

Eurich, N. P. *Corporate Classrooms: The Learning Business.* Princeton, N.J.: Carnegie Foundation for the Advancement of Teaching, 1985.

Feiman-Nemser, S., and Floden, R. E. "The Cultures of Teaching." In M. C. Wittrock (ed.), *Handbook of Research on Teaching.* (3rd ed.) New York: Macmillan, 1986.

Ferver, J. C. "Introduction to Coordinating SCDE Programs." *Journal of Research and Development in Education*, 1981, *15*, 22–72.

Fingeret, A. "Who's in Control? A Case Study of University-Industry Cooperation." In H. W. Beder (ed.), *Realizing the Potential of Interorganizational Cooperation.* New Directions for Continuing Education, no. 23. San Francisco: Jossey-Bass, 1984.

Flexner, A. "Is Social Work a Profession?" *School and Society*, 1915, *1*, 901–911.

Fox, R. D. "Formal Organizational Structure and Participation in Planning Continuing Professional Education." *Adult Education*, 1981, *31*, 209–226.

Friedson, E. *Professional Powers.* Chicago: University of Chicago Press, 1986.

Galper, J. H. *The Politics of Social Services.* Englewood Cliffs, N.J.: Prentice-Hall, 1975.

Getzels, J. W. "Problem Finding: A Theoretical Note." *Cognitive Science*, 1979, *3*, 167–172.

Giles, B. A. "Internal-External Locus of Control and Its Effects on Levels of Participation in Continuing Professional Education for Engineers." Unpublished doctoral dissertation, Graduate School of Education and Human Development, University of Rochester, 1985.

Ginzberg, E. "The Professionalization of the U.S. Labor Force." *Scientific American*, 1979, *240*, 48–53.

Giroux, H. A., and McLaren, P. "Teacher Education and the Politics of Engagement: The Case for Democratic Schooling." *Harvard Educational Review*, 1986, *56*, 213–238.

Glaser, R. "Education and Thinking: The Role of Knowledge." *American Psychologist*, 1984, *39*, 93–104.

Glaser, R. "All's Well That Begins and Ends with Both Knowledge and Process: A Reply to Sternberg." *American Psychologist*, 1985, *40*, 573–574.

Glazer, N. "The Schools of the Minor Professions." *Minerva*, 1974, *10*, 346–364.

Glickman, C. D. *Supervision of Instruction: A Developmental Approach*. Boston: Allyn & Bacon, 1985.

Gonnella, J. S., and Zeleznik, C. "Strengthening the Relationship Between Professional Education and Performance." In S. M. Grabowski (ed.), *Strengthening Connections Between Education and Performance*. New Directions for Continuing Education, no. 18. San Francisco: Jossey-Bass, 1983.

Gosnell, D. J. "Evaluating Continuing Nursing Education." *The Journal of Continuing Education in Nursing*, 1985, *15*, 9–11.

Gouldner, A. W. *The Future of the Intellectuals and the Rise of the New Class*. London: Macmillan, 1979.

Green, J. S., and Walsh, P. I. "Impact Evaluation in Continuing Medical Education." In A. B. Knox (ed.), *Assessing the Impact of Continuing Education*. New Directions for Continuing Education, no. 3. San Francisco: Jossey-Bass, 1979.

Green, J. S., and others (eds.). *Continuing Education for the Health Professions: Developing, Managing, and Evaluating Programs for Maximum Impact on Patient Care*. San Francisco: Jossey-Bass, 1984.

Greene, M. "In Search of a Critical Pedagogy." *Harvard Educational Review*, 1986, *56*, 427–441.

Greenwood, E. "Attributes of a Profession." *Social Work*, 1957, *2*, 45–55.

Griffith, D. E. "Professional Continuing Education in Engineering." In M. R. Stern (ed.), *Power and Conflict in Continuing Professional Education*. Belmont, Calif.: Wadsworth, 1983.

Griffith, W. S. "Persistent Problems and Promising Prospects in Continuing Professional Education." In R. M. Cervero and C. L. Scanlan (eds.), *Problems and Prospects in Continuing Professional Education*. New Directions for Continuing Education, no. 27. San Francisco: Jossey-Bass, 1985.

Gronlund, N. E. *Constructing Achievement Tests.* (3rd ed.) Englewood Cliffs, N.J.: Prentice-Hall, 1982.

Gross, S. M. "Demographic Study of the Relationship of Continuing Pharmaceutical Education to Selected Attitudinal- and Competence-Related Criteria." *American Journal of Pharmaceutical Education,* 1976, *40,* 141–148.

Grotelueschen, A. D. "Program Evaluation." In A. B. Knox and Associates, *Developing, Administering, and Evaluating Adult Education.* San Francisco: Jossey-Bass, 1980.

Groteleuschen, A. D. "Assessing Professionals' Reasons for Participating in Continuing Education." In R. M. Cervero and C. L. Scanlan (eds.), *Problems and Prospects in Continuing Professional Education.* New Directions for Continuing Education, no. 27. San Francisco: Jossey-Bass, 1985.

Groteleuschen, A. D. *Quality Assurance in Continuing Professional Education.* Athens: Adult Education Department, University of Georgia, 1986.

Groteleuschen, A. D., Harnisch, D. L., and Kenny, W. R. *An Analysis of the Participation Reasons Scale Administered to Business Professionals.* Occasional Paper No. 7. Urbana: Office for the Study of Continuing Professional Education, University of Illinois at Urbana-Champaign, 1979a.

Groteleuschen, A. D., Harnisch, D. L., and Kenny, W. R. *Research on Reasons for Participation in Continuing Professional Education.* Occasional Paper No. 5. Urbana: Office for the Study of Continuing Professional Education, University of Illinois at Urbana-Champaign, 1979b.

Guba, E. G., and Lincoln, Y. S. *Effective Evaluation: Improving the Usefulness of Evaluation Results Through Responsive and Naturalistic Approaches.* San Francisco: Jossey-Bass, 1981.

Haag, W. B. *A Call to Action: A Report of the National Conference on Continuing Professional Education.* University Park: Pennsylvania State University, 1987.

Harnisch, D. L. "The Continuing Education Reasons of Veterinarians." Unpublished doctoral dissertation, College of Education, University of Illinois at Urbana-Champaign, 1980.

Haug, M. R. "The Deprofessionalization of Everyone?" *Sociological Focus,* 1975, *8,* 197–213.

Hayes, R. B., and others. "A Critical Appraisal of the Efficacy of Continuing Medical Education." *Journal of the American Medical Association*, 1984, *251*, 61 – 64.

Hazzard, G. W. "Continuing Education for Scientists and Engineers." In National Science Foundation (ed.), *Continuing Education in Science and Engineering.* Washington, D.C.: National Science Foundation, 1977.

Heraud, B. J. "Professionalism, Radicalism, and Social Change." *Sociological Review Monograph*, 1973, *20*, 85 – 101.

Hermosa, L. C. "Factors That Influence the Participation of Nurses in Continuing Education Compared with Other Health Professionals." Unpublished doctoral dissertation, Department of Instructional Development and Administration, Boston University, 1986.

Hohmann, L. "Professional Continuing Education." In H. J. Alford (ed.), *Power and Conflict in Continuing Education.* Belmont, Calif.: Wadsworth, 1980.

Holli, B. B. "Continuing Professional Learning: Involvement and Opinions of Dietitians." *Journal of the American Dietetic Association*, 1982, *81*, 53 – 57.

Hospital Research and Educational Trust. *Training and Continuing Education: A Handbook for Health Care Institutions.* Chicago: Hospital Research and Educational Trust, 1970.

Houle, C. O. *The Design of Education.* San Francisco: Jossey-Bass, 1972.

Houle, C. O. *Continuing Learning in the Professions.* San Francisco: Jossey-Bass, 1980.

Houle, C. O. "Possible Futures." In M. R. Stern (ed.), *Power and Conflict in Continuing Professional Education.* Belmont, Calif.: Wadsworth, 1983.

Houle, C. O., Cyphert, F., and Boggs, D. "Education for the Professions." *Theory Into Practice*, 1987, *26*, 87 – 93.

Houston, R. W., and Freiberg, J. H. "Perpetual Motion, Blindman's Bluff, and Inservice Education." *Journal of Teacher Education*, 1979, *30*, 7 – 8.

Hubbard, J. P. "The Work Environment and Innovation Following Continuing Professional Education." Unpublished doctoral dissertation, Department of Adult Education, University of Georgia, 1988.

Hutchison, D. J. "The Process of Planning Programs of Continuing Education for Health Manpower." In R. J. Blakely (ed.), *Fostering the Growing Need to Learn.* Rockville, Md.: Division of Regional Medical Services, U. S. Department of Health, Education and Welfare, 1983.

Illich, I. *Disabling Professions.* London: Martin Boyers, 1977.

Isenberg, D. J. "How Senior Managers Think." *Harvard Business Review,* 1984, *62,* 81 – 90.

Isenberg, D. J. "The Author Replies." *Harvard Business Review,* 1985, *63,* 185 – 186.

Isenberg, D. J. "Thinking and Managing: A Verbal Protocol Analysis of Managerial Problem Solving." *Academy of Management Journal,* 1986, *29,* 775 – 788.

Johnson, T. R. *Professions and Power.* London: Macmillan, 1972.

Kasaba, R., and Abato, B. *Scientific Design of a Hospital Training System.* Springfield, Va.: National Technical Information Service, 1971.

Katz, L. "Developmental Stages of Preschool Teachers." *The Elementary School Journal,* 1972, *23,* 50 – 54.

Kaufman, H. G. "Individual Differences, Early Work Challenge, and Participation in Continuing Education." *Journal of Applied Psychology,* 1975, *60,* 405 – 408.

Kaufman, H. G. "Factors Affecting the Relationship Between Continuing Education and Performance: A State-of-the-Art Review." In National Science Foundation (ed.), *Continuing Education in Science and Engineering.* Washington, D.C.: National Science Foundation, 1977.

Kenny, W. R. "Progress Planning and Accreditation." In R. M. Cervero and C. L. Scanlan (eds.), *Problems and Prospects in Continuing Professional Education.* New Directions for Continuing Education, no. 27. San Francisco: Jossey-Bass, 1985.

Kidder, L. H. *Research Methods in Social Relations.* (4th ed.) New York: Holt, Rinehart & Winston, 1981.

Kirk, R. J. *Building Quality into Continuing Education: A Guide to Lifelong Learning.* Rockville, Md.: LearnTech Publications, 1981.

Kirkpatrick, D. L. (ed.). *Evaluating Training Programs.* Madison, Wis.: American Society for Training and Development, 1975.

Kissam, P. C. "The Decline of Law School Professionalism." *University of Pennsylvania Law Review*, 1986, *134*, 251 – 324.

Kleinman, S. *Equals Before God: Seminarians as Humanistic Professionals.* Chicago: University of Chicago Press, 1984.

Klemp, G. O., and McClelland, D. C. "What Characterizes Intelligent Functioning Among Senior Managers?" In R. J. Sternberg and R. K. Wagner (eds.), *Practical Intelligence — Nature and Origins of Competence in the Everyday World.* New York: Cambridge University Press, 1986.

Knowles, M. S. *The Modern Practice of Adult Education.* Chicago: Association Press, 1980.

Knox, A. B. "Lifelong Self-Directed Education." In R. J. Blakely (ed.), *Fostering the Growing Need to Learn.* Rockville, Md.: Division of Regional Medical Services, U. S. Department of Health, Education and Welfare, 1973.

Knox, A. B. *Adult Development and Learning: A Handbook on Individual Growth and Competence in the Adult Years.* San Francisco: Jossey-Bass, 1977.

Knox, A. B. (ed.). *Assessing the Impact of Continuing Education.* New Directions for Continuing Education, no. 3. San Francisco: Jossey-Bass, 1979.

Knox, A. B. "The Continuing Education Agency and Its Parent Organization." In J. C. Votruba (ed.), *Strengthening Internal Support for Continuing Education.* New Directions for Continuing Education, no. 9. San Francisco: Jossey-Bass, 1981.

Knox, A. B. "Organizational Dynamics in Continuing Professional Education." *Adult Education*, 1982, *32*, 117 – 129.

Knox, A. B. "Evaluating Continuing Professional Education." In R. M. Cervero and C. L. Scanlan (eds.), *Problems and Prospects in Continuing Professional Education.* New Directions for Continuing Education, no. 27. San Francisco: Jossey-Bass, 1985a.

Knox, A. B. "Adult Learning and Proficiency." In D. A. Kleiber and M. L. Maehr (eds.), *Motivation and Adulthood.* Greenwich, Conn.: JAI Press, 1985b.

Knox, A. B. "Reducing Barriers to Participation in Continuing Education." *Lifelong Learning: An Omnibus of Practice and Research*, 1987, *10*, 7 – 9.

Knox, A. B., and Associates. *Developing, Administering, and Evaluating Adult Education.* San Francisco: Jossey-Bass, 1980.

Kost, R. J. "Competition and Innovation in Continuing Education." In H. J. Alford (ed.), *Power and Conflict in Continuing Education*. Belmont, Calif.: Wadsworth, 1980.

Kovalik, J. G. "Modes of Continuing Professional Education: A Test of Houle's Typology with Pastors." Unpublished doctoral dissertation, Department of Leadership and Educational Policy Studies, Northern Illinois University, 1986.

Lanzilotti, S. S., and others. "The Practice Integrated Learning Sequence: Linking Education with the Practice of Medicine." *Adult Education Quarterly*, 1986, *37*, 38–47.

Larson, M. S. *The Rise of Professionalism*. Berkeley: University of California Press, 1977.

Larson, M. S. "Professionalism: Rise and Fall." *International Journal of Health Services*, 1979, *9*, 607–627.

Lauffer, A. The Practice of Continuing Education in the Human Services. New York: McGraw-Hill, 1977.

Lauffer, A. *Doing Continuing Education and Staff Development*. New York: McGraw-Hill, 1978.

Lebold, M. M. "The Relationship Between Levels of Nursing Practice and Continuing Professional Learning Among Registered Nurses." Unpublished doctoral dissertation, Department of Leadership and Educational Policy Studies, Northern Illinois University, 1987.

LeBreton, P. P., and others (eds.). *The Evaluation of Continuing Education for Professionals: A Systems View*. Seattle: University of Washington, 1979.

Levine, H. G., Moore, D. E., and Pennington, F. C. "Evaluating Continuing Education Activities and Outcomes." In J. S. Green and others (eds.), *Continuing Education for the Health Professions: Developing, Managing, and Evaluating Programs for Maximum Impact on Patient Care*. San Francisco: Jossey-Bass, 1984.

Lindsay, C. A., Queeney, D. S., and Smutz, W. D. *A Model and Process for University/Professional Association Collaboration*. University Park: Pennsylvania State University, 1981.

Litwak, E., and Hylton, L. "Interorganizational Analysis: A Hypothesis on Coordinating Agencies." *Adminstrative Science Quarterly*, 1962, *6*, 395–420.

Lloyd, J. S., and Abrahamson, S. "Effectiveness of Continuing Medical Education: A Review of the Evidence." *Evaluation and the Health Professions,* 1979, *2,* 251 – 280.

Long, H. B. *Adult Learning.* New York: Cambridge University Press, 1983.

Lynn, K. S. "Introduction to the Issue 'The Professions.' " *Daedalus,* 1963, *92,* 649 – 654.

Lynton, E. A. "A Role for Colleges in Corporate Training and Development." In American Association for Higher Education (ed.), *Partnerships with Business and the Professions.* Washington, D.C.: American Association for Higher Education, 1981.

Lynton, E. A. "Higher Education's Role in Fostering Employee Education." *Educational Record,* 1983, *64,* 18 – 25.

McKnight, J. "The Professional Service Business." *Social Policy,* 1977, *8,* 110 – 116.

Macrina, D. M. "Continuing Professional Education Needs and Expectations of Health Educators." Unpublished doctoral dissertation, College of Education, University of Illinois at Urbana-Champaign, 1982.

Mager, R. F. *Preparing Instructional Objectives.* Belmont, Calif.: Fearon, 1975.

Manning, P. R., and others. "Continuing Medical Education: Linking the Community Hospital and the Medical School." *Journal of Medical Education,* 1979, *54,* 461 – 466.

Marrett, C. "On the Specification of Interorganizational Dimensions." *Sociology and Social Research,* 1971, *56,* 83 – 97.

Marsick, V. J. (ed.). *Learning in the Workplace.* Kent, England: Croom Helm, 1987.

Mergener, M. A., and Weinswig, M. H. "Motivations of Pharmacists for Participating in Continuing Education." *American Journal of Pharmaceutical Education,* 1979, *43,* 195 – 199.

Meyer, T. C. "Toward a Continuum in Medical Education." *Bulletin of the New York Academy of Medicine,* 1975, *51,* 719 – 726.

Millerson, G. *The Qualifying Associations.* London: Routledge & Kegan Paul, 1964.

Moore, W. E. *The Professions: Roles and Rules.* New York: Russell Sage Foundation, 1970.

Mulford, C. L. *Interorganizational Relations: Implications for Community Development.* New York: Human Sciences Press, 1984.

Munby, H. "Metaphors, Puzzles, and Teachers' Professional Knowledge." Paper presented at the annual conference of the American Educational Research Association, Washington, D.C., April 1987.

Murphy, S. "Resistance in the Professions: Adult Education and the New Paradigms of Power." Unpublished doctoral dissertation, Department of Leadership and Educational Policy Studies, Northern Illinois University, 1986.

Nadler, L. *Corporate Human Resource Development.* New York: Van Nostrand Reinhold, 1980.

Nadler, L. (ed.). *The Handbook of Human Resource Development.* New York: Wiley, 1984.

Nadler, L., and Wiggs, G. D. *Managing Human Resource Development: A Practical Guide.* San Francisco: Jossey-Bass, 1986.

Naftulin, D. H., Ware, J. E., and Donnelly, F. A. "The Doctor Fox Lecture: A Paradigm of Educational Seduction." *Journal of Medical Education,* 1973, *48,* 630–635.

National University Continuing Education Association. *The Role of Colleges and Universities in Continuing Professional Education.* Washington, D.C.: National University Continuing Education Association, 1984.

Neves, D. M., and Anderson, J. R. "Knowledge Compilation: Mechanisms for Automatization of Cognitive Skills." In J. R. Anderson (ed.), *Cognitive Skills and Their Acquisition.* Hillsdale, N.J.: Lawrence Erlbaum Associates, 1981.

Nevo, D. "The Conceptualization of Educational Evaluation: An Analytical Review of the Literature." *Review of Educational Research,* 1983, *53,* 117–128.

Nowlen, P. M. *A New Approach to Continuing Education for Business and the Professions: The Performance Model.* New York: Macmillan, 1988.

Nowlen, P. M., and Stern, M. S. "Partnerships in Continuing Education for Professionals." In American Association for Higher Education (ed.), *Partnerships with Business and the Professions.* Washington, D.C.: American Association for Higher Education, 1981.

O'Conner, A. B. "Reasons Nurses Participate in Continuing Education." *Nursing Research,* 1979, *28,* 354–359.

Oddi, L. F. "Development of an Instrument to Measure Self-

Directed Continuing Learning." Unpublished doctoral dissertation, Department of Leadership and Educational Policy Studies, Northern Illinois University, 1984.

Oddi, L. F. "Development and Validation of an Instrument to Identify Self-Directed Continuing Learners." *Adult Education Quarterly*, 1986, *36*, 97 – 107.

Oddi, L. F. "Perspectives on Self-Directed Learning." *Adult Education Quarterly*, 1987, *38*, 21 – 31.

Parsons, T. *Essays in Sociological Theory*. New York: Free Press, 1949.

Patton, M. C. *Utilization-Focused Evaluation*. Beverly Hills, Calif.: Sage, 1978.

Pennington, F. C., and Green, J. "Comparative Analysis of Program Development Processes in Six Professions." *Adult Education*, 1976, *27*, 13 – 23.

Perrucci, R. "In the Service of Man: Radical Movements in the Professions." *Sociological Review Monograph*, 1973, *20*, 179 – 194.

Peters, T. J., and Waterman, R. H., Jr. *In Search of Excellence*. New York: Harper & Row, 1982.

Phillips, L. E. "Trends in State Relicensure." In M. R. Stern (ed.), *Power and Conflict in Continuing Professional Education*. Belmont, Calif.: Wadsworth, 1983.

Phillips, L. E. "Is Mandatory Continuing Education Working?" *Mobius*, 1987, *7*, 57 – 64.

Polancic, J. E. "A Factor Analytic Test of Houle's Typology of Professionals' Modes of Learning Utilizing Clinical Laboratory Professionals' Learning Activities." Unpublished master's thesis, Department of Leadership and Educational Policy Studies, Northern Illinois University, 1987.

Popiel, E. S. (ed.). *Nursing and the Process of Continuing Education*. (2nd ed.) St. Louis, Mo.: Mosby, 1977.

Puetz, B. E. "The Role of the Professional Association in Continuing Education in Nursing." *The Journal of Continuing Education in Nursing*, 1985, *16*, 89 – 93.

Queeney, D. S. "The Role of the University in Continuing Professional Education." *Educational Record*, 1984, *65*, 13 – 17.

Queeney, D. S., and Smutz, W. D. "Enhancing the Performance of Professionals: The Practice Audit Model." In S. C. Willis and S. S. Dubin (eds.), *Contemporary Approaches to Professional Updating* (tentative title). San Francisco: Jossey-Bass, forthcoming.

Quinn, R. E. *Beyond Rational Management.* San Francisco: Jossey-Bass, 1988.

Rao, C. Z. "The Effect of a Continuing Professional Education Program on the Practice of Hemodialysis Nurses and Their Patient Outcomes." Unpublished doctoral dissertation, Department of Leadership and Educational Policy Studies, Northern Illinois University, 1988.

Raymond, M. R. "The Effectiveness of Continuing Education in the Health Professions: A Reanalysis of the Literature." Paper presented at the annual conference of American Educational Research Association, San Francisco, April 1986.

Resnik, L. B. "Mathematics and Science Learning: A New Conception." *Science,* 1983, *220,* 477–478.

Richards, R. K., and Cohen, R. M. "Why Physicians Attend Traditional CME Programs." *Journal of Medical Education,* 1980, *55,* 479–485.

Rizzuto, C. R. "Relationship of Career Saliency and Sex Role Orientation to Participation of Working Women in Education." Unpublished doctoral dissertation, Graduate School of Education, University of California, Los Angeles, 1983.

Rose, G. "Issues in Professionalism: British Social Work Triumphant." In F. D. Perlmutter (ed.), *A Design for Social Work Practice.* New York: Columbia University Press, 1974.

Rothman, R. A. "Deprofessionalization: The Case of Law in America." *Work and Occupations,* 1984, *11,* 183–206.

Rottet, S., and Cervero, R. M. "Clinical Evaluation of a Nursing Orientation Program." *Journal of Nursing Staff Development,* 1986, *3,* 110–114.

Ruder, S. K. "The Comparison of Mandatory or Voluntary Participation in Continuing Education on Nursing Performance." Unpublished doctoral dissertation, Department of Leadership and Educational Policy Studies, Northern Illinois University, 1987.

Rueschemeyer, D. "Doctors and Lawyers: A Comment on the Theory of Professions." *Canadian Review of Sociology and Anthropology,* 1964, *1,* 17–30.

Rumelhart, D. E., and Norman, D. A. "Analogical Processes in Learning." In J. R. Anderson (ed.), *Cognitive Skills and Their Acquisition*. Hillsdale, N.J.: Lawrence Erlbaum Associates, 1981.

Ryor, J., Shanker, A., and Sandefeur, J. T. "Three Perspectives on Inservice Education." *Journal of Teacher Education*, 1979, *30*, 13–29.

Sabia, D. R., and Wallulis, J. (eds.). *Changing Social Science: Critical Theory and Other Critical Perspectives*. Albany: State University of New York Press, 1983.

Scanlan, C. L. "Practicing with Purpose: Goals of Continuing Professional Education." In R. M. Cervero and C. L. Scanlan (eds.), *Problems and Prospects in Continuing Professional Education*. New Directions for Continuing Education, no. 27. San Francisco: Jossey-Bass, 1985.

Scanlan, C. L., and Darkenwald, G. G. "Identifying Deterrents to Participation in Continuing Education." *Adult Education Quarterly*, 1984, *34*, 155–166.

Schein, E. *Professional Education*. New York: McGraw-Hill, 1973.

Schermerhorn, J. R. "Determinants of Interorganizational Cooperation." *Academy of Management Journal*, 1975, *18*, 846–856.

Schön, D. A. *The Reflective Practitioner*. New York: Basic Books, 1983.

Schön, D. A. "Towards a New Epistemology of Practice: A Response to the Crisis of Professional Knowledge." In A. Thomas and E. W. Ploman (eds.), *Learning and Development: A Global Perspective*. Toronto: The Ontario Institute for Studies in Education, 1985.

Schön, D. A. *Educating the Reflective Practitioner: Toward a New Design for Teaching and Learning in the Professions*. San Francisco: Jossey-Bass, 1987.

Schudson, M. "A Discussion of Magali Sarfatti Larson's *The Rise of Professionalism: A Sociological Analysis*." *Theory and Society*, 1980, *9*, 215–229.

Shanker, A. "The Making of a Profession." *American Educator*, 1985, *9*, 10–17, 46, 48.

Shelton, H. R., and Craig, R. L. "Continuing Professional Development: The Employer's Perspective." In M. R. Stern (ed.), *Power and Conflict in Continuing Professional Education.* Belmont, Calif.: Wadsworth, 1983.

Shuell, T. J. "Cognitive Conceptions of Learning." *Review of Educational Research,* 1986, *56,* 411–436.

Shulman, L. S. "Those Who Understand: Knowledge Growth in Teaching." *Educational Researcher,* 1986, *15,* 4–14

Simerly, R. G. "Achieving Success in Strategic Planning." In R. G. Simerly and Associates, *Strategic Planning and Leadership in Continuing Education: Enhancing Organizational Vitality, Responsiveness, and Identity.* San Francisco: Jossey-Bass, 1987.

Simerly, R. G., and Associates. *Strategic Planning and Leadership in Continuing Education.* San Francisco: Jossey-Bass, 1987.

Sjogren, D. D. "Issues in Assessing Educational Impact." In A. B. Knox (ed.), *Assessing the Impact of Continuing Education.* New Directions for Continuing Education, no. 3. San Francisco: Jossey-Bass, 1979.

Sleicher, M. N. "Nursing Is Not a Profession." *Nursing and Health Care,* 1981, *2,* 186–191, 218.

Smith, C. E. "Planning, Implementing, and Evaluating Learning Experiences for Adults." *Nurse Educator,* 1978, *3,* 31–36.

Smutz, W. D., Crowe, M. B., and Lindsay, C. A. "Emerging Perspectives on Continuing Professional Education." In J. C. Smart (ed.), *Higher Education: Handbook of Theory and Research.* Vol. 2. New York: Agathon Press, 1986.

Smutz, W. D., and Toombs, W. "Forming University/Professional Association Collaborative Relationships: The Strategic Selection of Boundary Spanners." Paper presented at the annual conference of the American Educational Research Association, Chicago, April 1985.

Smutz, W. D., and others. *The Practice Audit Model: A Process for Continuing Professional Education Needs Assessment and Program Development.* University Park: Pennsylvania State University, 1981.

Sneed, J. T. "Continuing Education in the Professions." *The Journal of Higher Education,* 1972, *43,* 223–238.

Sockett, H. T. "Has Shulman Got the Strategy Right?" *Harvard Educational Review,* 1987, *57,* 208–219.

Sork, T. J. "Programming in Continuing Professional Educa-

180

References

tion: A Comparative Analysis of Approaches to Planning." *Canadian Journal of University Continuing Education,* 1983, *9* (2), 48–57.

Sork, T. J., and Busky, J. H. "A Descriptive and Evaluative Analysis of Program Planning Literature, 1950–1983." *Adult Education Quarterly,* 1986, *36,* 86–96.

Sork, T. J., Kalef, R., and Worsfold, N. E. *The Postmortem Audit: A Strategy for Improving Educational Programs.* Vancouver, British Columbia: Educational Design Associates, 1987.

Spikes, F. "A Multidimensional Program Planning Model for Continuing Nursing Education." *Lifelong Learning: The Adult Years,* 1978a, *1,* 4–8.

Spikes, F. "Planning Continuing Nursing Education Programs: A Guide for the Practitioner." *The Journal of Continuing Education in Nursing,* 1978b, *9,* 5–10.

Staropoli, C. J., and Waltz, C. F. *Developing and Evaluating Educational Programs for Health Care Providers.* Philadelphia: F. A. Davis, 1978.

Stearns, N. S., Getchell, M. E., and Gold, R. A. *Continuing Medical Education in Community Hospitals: A Manual for Program Development.* Boston: Massachusetts Medical Society, 1971.

Stern, M. R. "Universities in Continuing Education." In H. J. Alford (ed.), *Power and Conflict in Continuing Education.* Belmont, Calif.: Wadsworth, 1980.

Stern, M. R. (ed.). *Power and Conflict in Continuing Professional Education.* Belmont, Calif.: Wadsworth, 1983a.

Stern, M. R. "A Disorderly Market." In M. R. Stern (ed.), *Power and Conflict in Continuing Professional Education.* Belmont, Calif.: Wadsworth, 1983b.

Sternberg, R. J. "All's Well That Ends Well, but It's a Sad Tale That Begins at the End: A Reply to Glaser." *American Psychologist,* 1985, *40,* 571–573.

Stone, E. W. "The Growth of Continuing Education." *Library Trends,* 1986, *34,* 489-513.

Stross, J. K., and Harlan, W. R. "The Impact of Mandatory Continuing Medical Education." *Journal of the American Medical Association,* 1978, *239,* 2663–2666.

Stross, J. K., and Harlan, W. R. "Mandatory Continuing Medical Education Revisited." *Mobius,* 1987, *7,* 22–27.

Suchman, E. A. *Evaluation Research.* New York: Russell Sage Foundation, 1967.

Suleiman, A. "Private Enterprise: The Independent Provider." In M. R. Stern (ed.), *Power and Conflict in Continuing Professional Education.* Belmont, Calif.: Wadsworth, 1983.

Tobin, H. M., Wise, P.S.Y., and Hull, P. K. *The Process of Staff Development: Components for Change.* (2nd ed.) St. Louis, Mo.: Mosby, 1979.

Toombs, W., and Lindsay, C. "Departments and Professions: Institutionalizing Continuing Professional Education." Paper presented at the annual conference of the American Educational Research Association, San Francisco, April 1986.

Toombs, W., Lindsay, C., and Hettinger, G. "Modifying Faculty Roles to Institutionalize Continuing Professional Education." *Research in Higher Education,* 1985, *22,* 93–109.

Turner, C., and Hodge, M. N. "Occupations and Professions." In J. A. Jackson (ed.), *Professions and Professionalization.* Cambridge, England: Cambridge University Press, 1970.

Tyler, R. W. *Basic Principles of Curriculum and Instruction.* Chicago: University of Chicago Press, 1949.

Unger, R. M. *The Critical Legal Studies Movement.* Cambridge, Mass.: Harvard University Press, 1986.

Vernon, D. H. "Education for Proficiency: The Continuum." *Journal of Legal Education,* 1983, *33,* 559–569.

Vicere, A. A. "Creating Order from Chaos: Academic Integrity in Continuing Professional Education." *Adult Education Quarterly,* 1985, *35,* 229–239.

Vollmer, H. M., and Mills, D. L. (eds.). *Professionalization.* Englewood Cliffs, N.J.: Prentice-Hall, 1966.

Votruba, J. C. (ed.). *Strengthening Internal Support for Continuing Education.* New Directions for Continuing Education, no. 9. San Francisco: Jossey-Bass, 1981.

Wagner, R. K., and Sternberg, R. J. "Practical Intelligence in Real-World Pursuits: The Role of Tacit Knowledge." *Journal of Personality and Social Psychology,* 1985, *49,* 436–458.

Waldon, G. D. "Variables Related to Intent to Participate in Continuing Professional Education." Unpublished doctoral dissertation, Department of Counseling, Educational Psychology, and Special Education, Michigan State University, 1985.

Walizer, M. E. "The Professor and the Practitioner Think About Teaching." *Harvard Educational Review*, 1986, *56*, 520–526.

Walsh, P. L. "A Model for Planning Continuing Education for Impact." *Journal of Allied Health*, 1981, *10*, 101–106.

Warmuth, J. F. "In Search of the Impact of Continuing Education." *The Journal of Continuing Education in Nursing*, 1987, *18*, 4–7.

Weick, K. E. "Managerial Thought in the Context of Action." In S. Srivastva and Associates, *The Executive Mind: New Insights on Managerial Thought and Action*. San Francisco: Jossey-Bass, 1983.

Weinstein, L. M. "Employers in the Private Sector." In R. E. Anderson and E. S. Kasl (ed.), *The Costs and Financing of Adult Education and Training*. Lexington, Mass.: Heath, 1982.

Welch, S. D. *Communities of Resistance and Solidarity*. Maryknoll, N.Y.: Orbis Books, 1985.

Whetten, D. "Interorganizational Relations: A Review of the Field." *Journal of Higher Education*, 1981, *52*, 1–28.

Wilensky, H. L. "The Professionalization of Everyone?" *American Journal of Sociology*, 1964, *70*, 137–158.

Worthen, B. R., and Sanders, J. R. *Educational Evaluation: Theory and Practice*. Belmont, Calif.: Wadsworth, 1973.

Younghouse, R. H., and Young, W. H. "Program Relationships of Community Hospitals and Medical Schools in CME." *Journal of Medical Education*, *59*, 553–558.

INDEX

183

184

viders for, 84; instructional strategies for, 51–52; intuition used by, 51; participation in educative activities of, 65; program planning model for, 120–121
Busky, J. H., 113, 114, 116

C

Canadian Journal of University Continuing Education, 15
Carroll, J. W., 42
Catlin, D. W., 65
Cervero, R. M.: categories of program evaluation questions, 134–146; on collaboration, 95–96, 109; interorganizational relationships in continuing professional education, 94–95, 105; on professional educative activities, 59, 61–62, 65, 68; typology of organizational interdependence of, 96, 99, 106
Charters, A. N., 119
Clark, C. M., 52
Clegg, W. H., 136
Clergy: career stages of, 70; conflicting values in, 34; deprofessionalization of, 7; participation in educative activities of, 61–62
Cognitive psychology: as basis of professional learning, 39–42, 50–51; continuing professional education and, 55–56
Cohen, R. M., 64
Cole, H. P., 141
Collert, M. E., 119
Colliver, J. A., 73, 74
Conflict viewpoint, 26–29; educational implications of, 29, 150; power as basis of, 27, 28, 29; social conflict in, 28–29, 30
Continuing professional education: adult education concepts and, 16; comparative approach to, 14–15; content decisions in, 36; criteria, 20–21; frames of reference for, 15–16; goals of institutions related to, 90–91, 93; growth and development of, 2; history of, 1–5; human resource development and, 16; in-

stitutional approaches to, 75–76, 93; mandatory, 2, 73–74; market of institutions related to, 92–93; means and ends of, 36, 37; performance as goal of, 25–26; practical knowledge fostered through, 55–56; procedural knowledge fostered through, 55; for the professions, 3–5; provided by employing agencies, 77, 84–86, 88; provided by independent providers, 77, 86–87, 88; provided by institutions, 76–78; provided by professional associations, 77, 78, 82–84, 88; provided by professional schools, 77, 78–79, 88; provided by universities, 77, 78, 79–82, 88; role in society of, 36; shortcomings of, 2–3; similarities in, 14–15, 16–17; technical process in, 25–26; theory and research for, 3. *See also* Educational activities, participation in; Educational providers
Continuing Professional Education Development Project, 101–102, 108
Continuing professional education effective practice, 4–5, 149–152; contextual basis of, 154–156; elements of, 150–152; epistemological basis of, 156–158; ethical basis of, 152–154; improving, 158–160; understanding, 152–158
Continuing professional education programs: evaluation of, 131–132
Continuing professional educators: institutional settings of, 75–76, 89; interest groups, 3; role in society of, 20; self-directedness in learning of, 69; training of, 4
Cooper, S. S., 118
Cordray, D. S., 134
Craig, R. L., 84, 103
Critical viewpoint, 29–37; conflicting values in, 33–35, 151–152; dialectic approach in, 30–32; educational implications of, 35–36, 150; model of learner based on, 54, 55; necessity for, 37
Cross, K. P.: on adult education, 64,

Index